Buying French Wine
from the
Château and Vineyard

AN EXPLORER'S GUIDE

Buying French Wine from the Château and Vineyard

AN EXPLORER'S GUIDE

HILARY WRIGHT

RESEARCH, MAPS AND INSPIRATION: IAN WRIGHT

MANDARIN

First published in Great Britain in 1994
by Mandarin Paperbacks
an imprint of Reed Consumer Books Limited,
Michelin House, 81 Fulham Road
London SW3 6RB
and Auckland, Melbourne, Singapore and Toronto

ISBN 0 7493 1819 8

Although all reasonable care has been taken in the preparation of this book, neither the
author nor the publishers can accept liability for any consequences arising from the
information contained herein, or from the use thereof.

A CIP catalogue record for this book is available from the British Library

Executive Editor: Anne Ryland
Art Director: Jacqui Small
Editor: Anthea Snow
Art Editor: Mark Winwood
Index: Ann Barrett
Map artwork: Bob Reed
Production: Michelle Thomas

Printed and bound in Great Britain by Cox & Wyman, Reading
Typeset in Monotype Bembo, Gill Sans and Palatino

Contents

How to Use this Book.............7

Introduction.........................**9**

Why Buy Wine in France? 9

When to Go...........................11

Planning the Route 14

Booking and
    Where to Stay................17

How to Buy Direct: You *Can*
    Survive a Tasting 19

How to Taste 21

A Note on Winemaking.......25

To Buy or Not to Buy 28

Bringing the Wine Home.....30

Getting Around,
    Getting Along.................33

Wine Rules and
    Regulations...................35

The Loire Valley.................**40**

The Pays Nantais..................43

Anjou-Saumur.......................51

Touraine 64

Burgundy **78**

Champagne **117**

Alsace...............................**142**

The Golden Triangle.......**172**

The Aube 173

Chablis 181

Sancerre and
    Pouilly-sur-Loire 188

Ferry Factfile....................**197**

Further Exploration
    DIY visits.....................**203**

Index 206

Maps

**The Wine Regions of
Northern & Central France** 8

The Loire Valley
The Pays Nantais 46
Anjou-Saumur...............................52
Touraine...................................65, 69

Burgundy 89

Champagne 131

Alsace...150

The Golden Triangle
The Aube 173
Chablis 183
Sancerre & Pouilly-sur-Loire 190

Abbreviations and Symbols

ha	hectares (1 hectare = 2.47 acres)
hl	hectolitres
cl	centilitres
km	kilometres
kg	kilograms
M	millions
FF	French francs
H	hotel
R	restaurant
♥	wine producer

A Note on Producers, Prices and Opening Hours

All prices and opening times quoted in this guide are based on information supplied in 1993 and are correct at the time of going to press. Do bear in mind, however, that the information may change before the date of your visit and telephoning ahead to confirm details and, if necessary, that English-speaking staff will be present, will avoid inconvenience. If you decide to travel with a party of friends, remember that the details of visits to producers apply only to small numbers of visitors, and many estates require an appointment to cater for a group.

Acknowledgments

Anne Dewe, Caroline Gestin, Christian Chabirand, Christine Whaite, Claire Duchene, Didier Krieg, Dominique Lambry, Edward Wright, Elizabeth Gabay, Elizabeth Powell, John P Harris, Joyce Wright, Kate Teesdale, Martine Greslom, Michael Edwards, Monique Denoune, Pat Lapins, Roselyne Delaunay, Sam Gordon Clark, Sandrine Perroud, Sophie Vallejo, Véronique Vallenot.

How to Use this Book

This guide shows you how to venture with confidence into the French wine regions to buy your wine direct from the people who make it, while enjoying good food and accommodation and the pleasures of travelling in rural France.

The Introduction gives practical information on everything from how to plan the journey and book accommodation, to what to expect when visiting a winemaker and how to taste wine and discover what you enjoy most. There's a concise description of the winemaking process to help you understand what you'll encounter in the cellar, and guidance on buying the wine and bringing it home safely.

Each of the next five chapters describes a wine route for you to follow, with recommended producers to visit and places to stay and enjoy local food; each gives information on how to get there – perhaps linking together one or more of the routes – and on the different styles of wine and winemaking practices you'll come across. The last of these chapters, The Golden Triangle, joins part of Burgundy, Champagne and the Loire Valley together in one easy route.

Each wine route is illustrated with one or more maps indicating with the symbols ♥, *H* and *R* where the recommended wine producers, hotels and restaurants described in the text are located. At the end of each of the regional chapters is a Listings section giving the addresses and telephone numbers of the winemakers, hotels and restaurants, as well as opening hours for the producers and details of the price of hotel rooms and restaurant meals.

The Ferry Factfile looks at the best routes for crossing the Channel, and is followed by advice on exploring in wine country on your own.

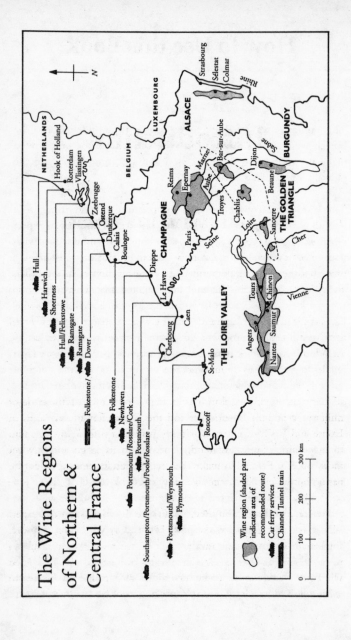

The Wine Regions
of Northern &
Central France

Introduction

WHY BUY WINE IN FRANCE?

I think everyone's heard by now about the amazing cheapness of wine bought in French supermarkets. Bargains can be had by anyone prepared to cross the Channel for the morning. This stupendous offer is brought to you courtesy of the British government, which has denied British wine merchants the chance to compete on equal terms with the French. Our duty laws impose over £1 in tax on each bottle we buy (the exact amount varies from budget to budget) while the French pay about tuppence.

So we cross the Channel in droves, depriving the UK wine trade of millions of pounds in turnover and the Chancellor of vast sums in Excise and VAT revenue. Obviously it's not a sufficiently vast sum to make him change his mind, so it's up to us to go and buy yet more wine in France, to make the revenue lost so enormous that he has no option but to 'harmonize' duty rates.

And even then I'd still buy wine in France. It would still be cheaper. Maybe not in the supermarket, but I don't buy wine there anyway. French supermarket wine isn't a patch on what we have available to us in the UK high street. We have teams of hideously well qualified wine buyers in every supermarket and off-licence chain, dedicated to sniffing out wines from every producing country in the world. In

France they have no need of this. Why seek out wines from all around the world when you consider its products inferior to your own? The French are notoriously parochial about the wines they drink, and frankly if I lived there I would be too. If you've got the best wine in the world on your doorstep, they argue, why look further afield.

You won't find the great wines of France in their supermarkets because people tend to buy direct from growers. They'll go to a wine region for the weekend and buy a few cases or arrange for a year's supply to be delivered. They make contact with a grower and build up a personal relationship. Dinner party conversations centre around 'my' winegrower – much more fun than drinking an impersonal bottle from a supermarket shelf.

Wouldn't it be wonderful to be able to turn up at a vineyard and arrange for 20 cases to be sent home to you? And at vineyard prices? There are UK haulage firms which would be happy to transport your wine to your door for as little as £3 a case. Unfortunately your friends the UK Customs and Excise take the view that this is a commercial transaction as you are not accompanying the goods, and will levy the full £1-plus duty per bottle. You must import the wine yourself.

So let's do as the French do: visit châteaux and vineyards, make direct contact with winemakers and buy wine at astonishing prices. For this is where the real bargains are to be had. My rule of thumb is that you can buy a bottle in the vineyard for about half what you'd pay in the UK high street. This applies just as much to bottles costing £3 as to those at £6; whatever you like to spend on average on a bottle of wine you'll find a bargain in your price range.

Now I know that in order to enjoy these prices you have to spend money – on ferries, petrol, hotels and restaurants. But here again, events are moving in our favour. The opening of the Channel

Tunnel has prompted a flurry of price cuts among the ferry companies. They're particularly keen to encourage us to cross to France more frequently, and their new tariffs reflect this. Not that I need any encouragement.

Nostalgia isn't what it was, and neither are French hotel prices, but they still seem reasonable to those of us used to the high cost of British hotels. Then there's the enjoyment of travelling in France. Compared to our overcrowded roads, driving in France can be a pleasure. Motorways in particular are quiet (except around Paris, except in rush hour, except in the peak holiday season), largely because you have to pay tolls for the privilege of using them.

Eating in France is also a real pleasure. Sometimes I like to worship in temples of gastronomy, but more often I prefer the simpler cooking of small places with regional dishes and local customers. The value you can find in French restaurants, especially on the fixed-price menus, still amazes me. And the chance to experience a completely different rhythm of life for a few days entices me back again and again.

So although you can certainly argue that you don't save money on the trip as a whole, I'd argue that the experience as a whole knocks buying wine at Sainsbury's into a cocked hat.

WHEN TO GO

Next week. Next month. As soon as possible and as often as possible. Me, I don't need an excuse. But I do have certain rules of thumb: principally, never go to France in August. The French don't believe in off-season holidays. Their *vacances* run from mid-July to the end of August, and woe betide you if you travel on 'black Saturday', the day *la toute Paris* gets into its car and heads to all points south and/or coastal. Families tied to school holidays have no choice; but this book isn't about family holidays, it's about having fun (sorry).

September and October are without doubt the best times to travel to wine regions, to see the harvest. The excitement is almost palpable as tractors steam firmly down the middle of the road, trailers overflowing with grapes. Teams of pickers trudge between rows of vines, their caravans snaked around the edges of fields like wagon trains. Walking through villages, the heady smell of fermentation is everywhere. The two or three weeks of harvest are the culmination of a whole year's work; mistakes now, or bad weather, can severely reduce the year's income. No wonder it's a fraught, hectic time. I adore it.

It's the best of times and the worst of times. The best because you can see all the machinery in operation: conveyor belts loading grapes into the press, juice pouring out of the press as it turns, open fermentation vats frothing away. Suddenly all the theory of how wine is made makes sense, it all comes together. The downside, of course, is that the winemakers are much too busy actually making the stuff to talk to you about it.

Many small-scale growers don't accept visitors at all during the harvest, or if they do they have much-reduced time to talk to you. Some larger firms, on the other hand, positively welcome you at this time and will proudly show you all the processes in detail. It really pays to contact growers in advance if you plan to visit during the harvest. You won't waste time trying to see people who are too busy to help you, and you'll learn a lot from those who <u>are</u> geared up to receive you – especially if you're expected.

Late autumn and winter, when the harvest is safely gathered in and bubbling away in the cellars, is a good time to go. Winemakers have more time for you (any excuse to put off pruning the vines in biting winds and sub-zero temperatures). Note, though, that many hotels close for a month or more in winter: January can be a lean month for accommodation. Spring and early summer, as the buds break on the vine and the flowers develop, also have their attractions, not least the better weather.

It makes sense to travel light if you're going to buy wine. Excess luggage reduces your payload. So do excess passengers. Although it may be fun to travel in a foursome, you won't have much room in a family saloon to bring back much wine. In particular, children with all their paraphernalia take up a great deal of room. Also, children have a different agenda, and trudging round estates and watching you taste something they probably don't like is unlikely to feature highly on it. So this seems like the best possible excuse to leave the children for a weekend with the grandparents, or indeed anyone who'll have them, and take off on your own, otherwise you may find your loyalties split. I heard a story in Chablis about a prominent British newsreader who packed his two children off home by train in order to free their seats for extra cases of wine in the back of his Volvo.

How long you go for is of course determined by both time and financial constraints. The visits to wine regions I describe in the following chapters, each of which guides you along a wine route, can be made in a long weekend, reckoned as five days, taking advantage of the ferry companies' five-day return ticket. It's easy to extend the itineraries if you have more time as there are plenty of estates to visit and sights to see. The routes are also modular, so that if you have more time you can join one or two wine regions together and stay for as long as you can manage.

The decision on where to go can be determined by the kind of wine you prefer, your desire to explore, or your fondness or otherwise for encountering your fellow countrymen and countrywomen while abroad. The Loire Valley and Champagne are certainly the most popular regions with Brits, and a fair number get down to Burgundy, but Alsace sees relatively few British cars (Germany and Scandinavia make up for this).

Most of the regions covered in this guide produce mainly white wine. This should suit the British as 70% of the wine consumed in the UK is white. It's not surprising that whites should predominate, as black grapes find it harder to ripen in chilly northern climates. However, all the regions discussed, not only Burgundy, make some red wine, and I'll tell you where to find it.

This book concentrates exclusively on the four wine regions nearest the Channel ports: the Loire Valley, Champagne, Burgundy and Alsace. These are the easiest to reach, and less travel time means more time enjoying what's on offer. These are also regions which welcome visitors. Bordeaux is doing its best to shed its unfriendly reputation, and in a year or two might be more fun than the old suit-and-tie-and-by-appointment-only image suggested.

PLANNING THE ROUTE

There are three elements to consider: getting to the Channel port, choice of Channel transport, route to wine territory. The second element is likely to be determined by where you live. I'm fortunate to be living in Kent, which puts the majority of Channel transport on my doorstep; but when I first travelled to France I lived in Cumbria, and the journey to any Channel port from there is not undertaken lightly. Nor is the M25, and in particular the queue for the Dartford Tunnel, for the faint-hearted, although I believe that if I only travel on the M25 outside rush hour I'll never get caught in snarl-ups, and this has indeed been the case. (This is a very useful belief to have.)

For the north and Scotland, the Hull ferry to Zeebrugge is more useful than is at first apparent. To reach Burgundy and Alsace, the route via Brussels and Luxembourg down to Metz is, if anything, slightly shorter than going via Calais; and for Champagne, dropping south at Brussels to Reims is very straightforward. For southerners, Calais is the obvious port for these three regions. Portsmouth to Le Havre avoids London for Wales and the west of England but unfortunately you then have to contend with Paris.

To reach the Loire Valley, the situation is rather different. The western Channel crossings are an attractive option, especially if you want to take what airlines so inelegantly call an 'open-jaw' route, out on one crossing and back on another – perfectly permissible if you travel with the same company on both legs. This is a particularly good idea when exploring along the meandering Loire. From Calais, the Loire is a long slog. (Further details are in the Ferry Factfile.)

Once in France, three types of road are at your disposal. Motorways are called 'A' roads (for Autoroute) and offer a useful network, although heavily biased to routing you via Paris. These are toll roads, except on urban stretches. Expect to pay about FF200 one way from Calais to Strasbourg – they're not cheap.

A slower but more comprehensive network is provided by the 'N' roads: Routes Nationales. No tolls, but lots of heavy wagons. These are the main arterial roads, and personally I don't like using them. I prefer to get where I'm going on the motorway, then switch to 'D' roads for meandering once I'm there.

'D' is for Départemental, for roads administered by each separate county (*département*). Each county has its own numbering system, so expect to see many different D1s. These are strictly local roads, often surprisingly wide and quiet, which allow you to devise very attractive routes bypassing towns.

There are many touring maps of France available, but there's only one I give car room to, the Michelin. Published every July, it's a bang-up-to-date, accurate atlas. Make sure you travel with the latest edition, as France is still expanding its motorway network and building bypasses that could make quite a difference to your choice of route.

A new map should help you avoid what happened the first time I tried Continental navigation. Mainland Europe designates some of its motorways as long-distance euroroutes, signified by E numbers.

Attempting to navigate around Brussels, things went disastrously wrong until I realized that all the E roads had been renumbered. It caused severe marital disharmony until we bought a new map.

I prefer to buy the complete atlas, so that I can fantasize about visiting bits of France I haven't yet been to; others prefer to buy the maps as individual fold-out sheets as they're less cumbersome on your lap. (You can ensure the sheet maps are up-to-date by checking the year of printing, shown in tiny numbers on a corner of the cover.)

The other advantage of using Michelin is that the maps cross-refer with the guidebooks. I do think it's worth obtaining the red Michelin guide to French hotels and restaurants. I find its recommendations reliable and it contains masses of information not possible to include in this guide, such as when a hotel closes, because it changes each year. It can also help if you need an extra stopover en route. If you want to navigate in towns, Michelin red guides are particularly helpful. In the atlas, a red box is drawn around major towns. The area covered by the box is mapped in detail in the red guide.

Other purchases to make before you leave include personal and car insurance – and pick up a reciprocal health treatment E111 form from the Post Office. Many insurance companies offer a free green card as part of the package, which is well worth having. Car recovery and personal insurance are vital, in my opinion, and it's worth shopping around on price. If you intend to make several trips in a year it'll pay you to take out an annual policy, such as that offered by Europ Assistance. The RAC offers vehicle recovery throughout Europe as an add-on to its usual package, but you still have to arrange personal cover. I found last year that this arrangement didn't work out as competitive as a full annual policy.

Another preparation you must make is to adjust your headlight beam. This usually involves blanking off a small part of the headlight lens using a rather pricey kit with various adhesive black plastic shapes. You can see the area to be covered up clearly outlined on the headlamp. The Wright Patent Gaffer-Tape Method (also known as the oh-drat-I-forgot-to-buy-that-blanking-out-kit technique) involves cutting a piece of gaffer tape to fit the outline and sticking it on. This can also work with black electrical tape. Make sure the surface is dry first. A more sophisticated solution is provided by clear plastic reflectors, which cost about £5 from the AA. These deflect your beam, rather than masking it, and if you intend to do a lot of night or winter driving will give you much better light. They're supposed to be re-usable; when I tried them one nearly fell off after a week and the other was almost impossible to dislodge, requiring a sharp knife (and breaking in the process).

Check with your insurance company what other equipment you need to take, such as spare bulbs and fire extinguishers, as the legal requirements change from time to time.

A final note: petrol is dearer in France than in Britain, so cross the Channel with a full tank. Petrol is cheapest in Luxembourg, however, so contrive to fill up there if you can. French credit card machines occasionally refuse to read UK credit cards (French cards now contain a microchip). On the one occasion this happened to me, a slip was made out manually. Ask the shop to swipe the magnetic band rather than read the chip.

BOOKING AND WHERE TO STAY

There's a great deal to be said for spur-of-the-moment, go-as-you-please trips, where you potter idly along until you find somewhere you'd care to rest for the night. Great idea, and a lot of fun, but I wouldn't recommend it when going to buy wine. Especially if you have to travel at weekends. Chablis, for instance, is only a couple of hours' drive from Paris and not much further from Brussels. Parisiens have just the same pleasure in buying direct as we do, so ensure your accommodation is booked well in advance. At weekends and after 8pm, economy telephone rates prevail; and it doesn't take a long call to say: 'Have you got a room with a bath on the 25th?'.

I've never confirmed by letter, and I've never had a mix-up with bookings, although that doesn't mean it doesn't happen. These days I often confirm with a short fax – but I never book that way. I feel much safer sorting out everything on the phone first, using paper only to confirm what's already been agreed. Sometimes I book the first night or two from the UK and the rest on the road. (Many French phone boxes use phonecards, *télécartes*, available from tobacconists, petrol stations etc. They're also useful for phoning ahead to producers.)

There are several hotel chains and associations in France. Some chains, such as Novotel and Campanile, are handily situated near main routes on the edge of towns, all based on exactly the same design and offering a good level of comfort, if rather functional. Then there are groupings of independent hotels. The most widespread of these is Logis de France, made up of small- to medium-sized family-run concerns. These are often furnished in 'traditional' style, featuring heavy furniture and loud floral wallpaper on every available surface including furniture panels and ceilings. Plumbing may be idiosyncratic, which all adds to the fun – no two hotels are alike. The association encourages regional cooking among its members and organizes an annual competition. The Logis guide is published annually (not free, alas, it costs about £8 from bookshops or the French Tourist Office).

At the other end of the scale is the Relais et Châteaux group. Its brochures come complete with a colour photo of each establishment, and members are often firmly in the luxury class. Some are temples of gastronomy, others merely pretentious. In between lies Relais du Silence which, as you might imagine, concentrates on tranquil locations. Prices are closer to those of Logis than those of Relais et Châteaux.

One important difference between French and British hotels is that in France it's common to have a weekly closing day. I remember trying to explain this to an American colleague and being met with a look of blank disbelief. Restaurants frequently close on Sunday night, after serving a blow-out Sunday lunch, and may not reopen until Tuesday. Hotels may do the same. Monday night accounts for a disproportionately high number of closures, so if your trip includes one, plan well ahead.

When booking, note that the price quoted is per room, not per person, and doesn't include breakfast. This is usually brought to your room on a tray on demand, but you're under no obligation to order it. Sometimes you can be charged FF50 for little more than coffee, bread and jam. If you're in a town, there's nothing to stop you nipping out for breakfast in a local café. It's half the price, and you get to see the world going by.

When you arrive at a hotel it's normal practice to inspect the room before accepting it, and it's perfectly OK to ask to see something bigger or better if you wish. I still remember the buzz I got after doing this for the first time – the second room I was offered was superb. Hoteliers often hold back their best rooms, so don't be afraid to ask.

HOW TO BUY DIRECT

YOU *CAN* SURVIVE A TASTING

It can be very easy: walk in, taste a couple of bottles, flash the plastic, walk out with a couple of cases. Put at its simplest, that's all you do. But it can be much more involved, with visits to the cellar or out into the vineyards, and an explanation of the winemaker's philosophy and the styles of wine available in the region which could run into an hour or two. For me, that's what makes it fun, and that's how I learned about the wines of France. There is absolutely nothing like being in the region and visiting the growers to enable you to understand the wines. In fact, I'd go so far as to say it's the only way to make a wine region truly come alive.

Naturally, if you walk into someone's cellar, the selection on offer will be limited to what the winemaker produces. In particular, it's important to realize that not all the wines on sale will necessarily be ready to drink. A generalization: the dearer the wine, the longer you need to keep it. Like all generalizations, this isn't true in every case; wines made from Sauvignon Blanc, for instance, need to be drunk young, which is handy to know when buying in Sancerre. But in Alsace, the finest Rieslings will benefit from several years in bottle, whereas the cheaper ones are designed to be drunk more or less straight away. The French way of buying direct is to lay in sufficient quantities to enable you to keep the wine until it's ready to drink, opening a bottle every now and again to check on progress.

Who will you meet? In smaller properties, usually the winegrower himself (in most cases, but not always, it's a man) or his spouse. Often husband and wife teams will split the work so that he's outside with the grapes and she's inside with the paperwork and visitors. You set the pace. If all you want to do is quietly taste a couple of bottles, they'll let you get on with it. If you want to know more, they'll gladly answer your questions. The pride people take in their wines quickly becomes evident, so it's important to treat the wines you're offered with proper respect.

You may be received in a large, commercial tasting-room or in what feels like the front parlour. You may be invited to sit at a table, or there may simply be a long counter to stand round and be served at. Usually you're handed a price list, but there may be a noticeboard showing the range and prices. When you're asked what you want to taste, it may be easy, as there may only be a few wines on sale. If there's a big range, such as in Alsace, you can choose. You may want a selection from the range, which takes in all the grape varieties, or you may prefer to concentrate on a particular variety. You may be shopping for cheap wines or for dear wines.

The basic principle is to taste white before red, young before old, and dry before sweet. In practice the principle is also to taste cheap before dear; the more complex, expensive wines will, the theory goes, completely overwhelm your palate with their superior taste and intensity so that you can't then taste their more ordinary, cheaper cousins. It's helpful therefore to give an idea at the outset of what you want to taste, so that the pourer can offer the wines in the best order.

If you don't know what you'd like to try, feel free to say so. Most growers won't mind that you know nothing about their wines, or the wines of the region, and will be happy to take it from the top. (A few winemakers prefer not to do this, and want you to have some experience with wine. Where this is the case among the producers listed in this guide, I've made that plain in the write-up, so that you can pitch your visit with confidence.) All the growers I list welcome visitors; you won't find yourself being haughtily assessed by some chic château proprietor, nor do you have to turn up in a suit and tie (and if anyone mentioned here should give you an unfriendly welcome, I'd like to know about it).

HOW TO TASTE

So you've got the first wine in the glass. A tasting sample is small, enough for one or two mouthfuls. You don't need more than this to tell what the wine is like, and a small amount gives you plenty of room to swirl it about in the glass.

But first, contemplation. Look intently at the wine. Tilt it away from you against something white if the light is good enough, because that will give you the best idea of its colour and clarity. This is a good way to indicate your respect for the wine you're about to taste. What are you looking for? Colour can tell you about age and condition. To generalize again: in whites, the darker the wine the older and/or richer and sweeter it is. A wine that has been exposed to oak will be a little darker than one that hasn't. A young Muscadet will be very pale in colour, a mature oaky burgundy much richer and deeper. Late-harvest Alsace wines will be golden and almost viscous in texture. However, if air has leaked into the bottle via a faulty cork, it will have oxidized the wine and turned it gold before its time through premature ageing. Your nose will confirm this diagnosis by picking up 'off', dusty, fusty smells. Red wines move from purply-red when young to browny-red when mature. The lighter a red wine looks, the lighter-bodied it will be.

Once you've paid your visual respects, sniff the wine briefly to check it's in good condition. (If it's faulty, as described above, you won't want to inhale more of the pong than absolutely necessary.) Then swirl the glass vigorously. This brings air into contact with the wine, encouraging it to release its aromas. If the wine is too cold – often the case with reds straight from the cellar – warm it by cupping your hand around the base of the glass. Then stick your nose right into the glass and breathe in deeply. I often close my eyes at this point. Closing down vision releases the brain to concentrate on other senses – my nose needs all the help it can get. What does it smell like?

This is where wine-tasting gets very personal. What the smell reminds you of may mean nothing to anyone else. It's a subjective art, which happily means you can never be wrong if all you're doing is deciding on the right wine for you to buy. There is a useful check-list, however, of smells and tastes that many people have attached to particular grapes, handy for identification. They are:

Riesling (mature) oily, petrolly, often minerally
Gewürztraminer lychees, elderflower, turkish delight
Sauvignon Blanc gooseberries, cat's pee

Chenin Blanc wet wool
Pinot Noir manure
Cabernet Sauvignon blackcurrants
Cabernet Franc blackcurrants (but less intense); stalky, minty
Chardonnay (oaky) butter, vanilla, toast

You may find you disagree entirely with this list, and that's fine, because nobody knows what someone else's nose is telling them. What is helpful is to build up pictures or associations in your own mind about what particular varieties smell and taste like, as your own points of reference.

Finally, taste. Take a good mouthful and do with it all the things mother told you not to: draw in air over it, make gurgly noises, chew the wine, rub it over your gums. Do whatever you have to do to draw more air into the wine, encouraging it to release its taste, and then spread that taste all over your mouth to where the different taste receptors are. Then spit it out. Yes, really, not just the person who's driving. If you want to taste more than a handful of wines, the mouthfuls you swallow will blunt your tastebuds for the wines yet to come. You won't experience more of the wine if you swallow, the swirl and chew has alerted all the parts of you which can taste.

That's my rule, and I admit I break it all the time, especially in Champagne where nobody appears to spit, ever. And sometimes, at the end of a tasting when really classy wines are being poured, I simply can't resist swallowing them. Some growers consider it a real waste to spit out their lovely wine. If you see no spittoons, ask for one (*un crachoir*); they'll probably give you an ice bucket.

When tasting I prefer to avoid eye contact and I certainly don't want anyone talking in my ear, or I become completely distracted and forget what I thought about the wine. Turning away helps. Finally, having spat, I write down what I thought. This last is not essential, but it can be very useful if you're tasting lots of wines in various places, or you simply want a record to look back on – or you happen to be writing a book. It also gives you time to think if you're not sure about the wine.

Now you need to give some response to what you've tasted. In a large tasting-room, with many customers and pourers, there isn't much pressure to respond. When someone's giving you their personal attention, though, it's different. If they're looking at you expectantly an appreciative nod is always a good start. You may feel you don't have sufficient vocabulary to convey your opinion; don't let that put you off. It's said that 93% of what we communicate to others is non-verbal. By this reckoning, if you don't speak a word of French that puts you only 7% behind the native speakers.

If you can establish a rapport with the grower you'll find communication remarkably easy. If they're shy (and many small-scale growers are) there's no need to say much. If they're voluble and expressive, waving your arms about in similar fashion will help things along nicely. I know it sounds daft, but I've tried it and it works.

Most of us studied French at school and think we can't speak it; but with a little practice it's surprising how much can come back and find a useful purpose. We British have a dreadful reputation as linguists, and I could perhaps be accused of pandering to this by emphasizing those producers who speak English. But I believe it's a matter of confidence. I recommend producers who speak English as a starting-point for exploration. After a while it becomes easier to visit producers who don't speak English, and to branch out on your own. Rapport will help enormously.

If you have struck up a successful rapport you may even find yourself invited into the cellar to taste the wines still in cask. This is a great compliment to your interest in the grower's wines, to your knowledge and to your tasting ability, as you are being invited to assess wines still in development. The grower will extract wine from the cask through a tap at the bottom of the barrel or with a pipette. Definitely spit this after tasting – in a cellar it's normal practice to spit on the floor. Watch what the grower does with the untasted remains in the glass. Some will pour that on the ground too, others will carefully pour it back into the cask. If the latter is done, hand your glass back so that yours can be poured back into the vat as well.

A NOTE ON WINEMAKING

If you're taken on a tour of the cellars, you can learn a great deal about the winemaker's approach. Any cellar should be spotlessly clean, but some will be packed with shiny stainless steel towers and others full of dank wood, complete with black mould on the ceiling. Can this really be a hygienic place to produce wine?

The truth is that the black mould is a very good sign. It only grows when temperature (low) and humidity (high) are the optimum for maturing wine. Dank cellars are just what wine needs. But what about vinification itself – the process whereby grapes are made into wine? The producer has many options at each stage, beginning with the choice of press. Pneumatic ones, using pressure from an inflatable air-bag, are held to be the gentlest, but they're also the dearest. The gentler the pressure, the clearer the resultant grape juice or must. Now, let the must settle for 24–48 hours (*débourbage*) or filter it straight away? And can we design a cellar so that the must flows from one tank to another (the best method), or do we have to pump it?

Where will the must ferment? In stainless steel or wood? In small oak barrels or in larger, old wood vats? Stainless steel is very popular as a fermentation vessel because it enables you to control the wine's temperature. This can be done simply by pouring cold water down the outside of a tank to cool down a too-vigorous fermentation, or with sophisticated coils within the vat that can cool or heat the wine as required, all wired up to electronic control desks. Cool fermentation of white wine, at about 18–20°C (65–68°F), has caused a revolution in winemaking and is responsible for all those crisp, fresh, dry, neutral wines we buy in the UK for about £3.

You can't mess about with heating coils and electronic control panels that look like something out of Star Trek when you ferment your wine in a wooden vat. Nor are the post-Second World War vessels you'll see – glass fibre things or tiled concrete chambers – any use with the high tech approach. Winemakers using older or more traditional equipment may have less control over proceedings but they may like it that way, preferring to let the wine develop as Nature intended rather than intervening too much.

Some producers swear that barrel-fermentation makes a more elegant, structured wine. Wood is also prized for maturing wine in because it's slightly porous, allowing a small amount of air through to the wine as it matures. New barrels also add a woody taste, currently very fashionable in whites as well as reds. After a few years in use, say four or five, a barrel has given up all its 'woody' flavours, so wine placed in it to mature is not going to taste of wood, but simply bene-fit from controlled exposure to air. The downside of maturing wine in wood is that it evaporates. Producers lose money through having to top up the vats (you can't leave a gap above the wine, as this would allow too much exposure to air and the wine would oxidize). That's why many producers mature their wine in stainless steel.

What will be used to start fermentation? The natural yeasts found in the 'bloom' on the grapes, or specially-made cultured yeasts? The latter give you more control, the former, it's argued, the genuine taste of the grape and the vintage.

What temperature do you want to ferment at? For red wines, the higher the temperature, the more colour and tannin you'll extract. For whites and reds, the lower the temperature, the better the aromas, freshness and fruitiness. Too low, however, and the yeasts become dormant; the fermentation process then stops and is difficult to restart. Too high a temperature and the yeasts are killed off, with dire consequences. Light, aromatic whites are best fermented below 18°C (65°F), while heavier whites such as burgundy and Alsace may be better at 18–20°C (65–68°F). Red wines ferment at higher temperatures, say 25–30°C (77–86°F), so you'll probably want to keep them somewhere else during this stage.

Once the wine has finished fermenting, do you leave it on its lees – the spent yeast cells – to gain more flavour (as with Muscadet)? Or do you rack the wine (transfer it to a clean barrel, leaving any sediment behind)? Do you 'do the malo', a further, malolactic fermentation which converts sharp, appley malic acid into softer lactic acid? Do you leave it to mature – in which case for how long? Do you fine it (clarify it) or filter it?

The presence of other equipment, particularly a great deal of filtration apparatus, indicates an interventionist attitude. Filtration is a sad thing to inflict on a wine. You're removing tiny particles in suspension in the wine, and that's bound to detract, in however small a way, from the wine's taste. Unfortunately we consumers are partly responsible for this. We object to seeing 'bits' in a wine and think it's faulty, whereas usually the reverse is the case. In white wines, for instance, white tartrate crystals often appear. This is actually a sign of un-mucked-about-with wine, but so many people complain about it that many producers nearly freeze the wine after fermentation in order to precipitate the crystals before bottling, to stop us taking the bottles back.

A very few producers avoid filtration altogether. Others filter 'as gently as possible'. It's one of the questions you can ask which will tell you a great deal about winemakers' attitudes to their wines. Modern winemaking technology is extremely expensive, all that stainless steel and control equipment, for instance. Often it's only the larger estates which can afford it. Often, too, they're the ones which go for filtration in a major way. But take a good look round. What does the equipment you see tell you about the sort of wine that's made? Is it all tightly controlled and regulated, or is the attitude more laid-back, with the wine allowed to 'do its own thing', to follow a natural course? One thing's for sure – even the tiniest, oldest cellar should be scrupulously clean, with nowhere for harmful bacteria to lurk that could interfere with the wine.

Another invitation you may receive is to go into the vineyards. I always accept with alacrity; there's usually something to learn, and if you're lucky the view will be terrific. Here you can see at first hand what the soil is like, how the vines are grown, and where the site is located. (For more information about vineyard activities, see pages 35–9.)

TO BUY OR NOT TO BUY

So you've tasted the wines, you've seen the cellar perhaps or been out into the vineyards. It comes to the crunch – what are you going to buy? If you've paid for the tasting, then that was a commercial transaction which leaves you with no further obligation. You can say thank you and goodbye without a backward glance. But usually the producer has spent time with you explaining the wines and offering you several free glasses to taste. Although the producers listed below enjoy receiving visitors and explaining the regions and their wines, selling wine is their livelihood. It's only courteous to buy a couple of bottles at least, in acknowledgment of the time they've given you.

If you like the wine, and it's something you'd enjoy drinking at home, then buy it in sufficient quantity to give you pleasure. I'd say that six bottles was the minimum to allow you to enjoy the wine on different occasions with different foods, and to experience the changes in taste as the wine matures over months or years. One of the mistakes I made when I first started buying in France was to bring home just two or three bottles of a wine I liked. Even with six, I found that because I'd bought the wine before it was ready and started drinking it too soon, only the last bottle gave me any idea of what it really had to offer. And by then, of course, it was too late.

Wine-buying Brits used to be known as 'one-bottles'. I blame the dreadful old import laws, where we had to ration ourselves tightly to keep within the 12-bottle limit. Now, only our axles hold us back, and the pleasure of buying by the case direct from the people who make the wine is finally within our grasp. Grab it with both hands.

A growing number of estates accept Access and Visa (although very few take American Express), mainly because they know we buy more if we can use plastic. This information is given in the producer listings. The majority of estates, however, still don't accept credit cards so be prepared with Eurocheques, French franc traveller's cheques or ready money.

Once you've bought your wine you'll be given an invoice, a *facture*, showing details of the wine and the price paid. It will also make clear that you've paid the VAT. Hang on to this paperwork until you're back in the UK, just in case a marauding Excise inspector wants proof of what you've been up to. These invoices are required by French law of all wine that's on the move, and it's particularly important if you buy wine in containers other than labelled bottles. The invoice proves that what you've got in that plastic barrel is legitimate AC burgundy, say, and not something shady from over the border for surreptitious blending with the indigenous stuff.

Another way of discovering local wines is to check out your hotel's wine list. The establishment may very well make its own wine, and if it doesn't it will certainly have links with several local producers. Ask your waiter for a recommendation, and if you enjoy what you've been served, ask for the producer's address. The hotel may even make an appointment for you to see the winemaker, which should ensure a warm welcome. This is a great way to discover your own personal hot tip: it may be a rising star the wine press hasn't yet pounced on, or someone making wine in a very small way, part-time or as a hobby.

BRINGING THE WINE HOME

How much will the car hold? Tricky question, this. You can make all the experiments you like, fitting suitcases and boxes into the boot, but real life will be different. Your vehicle manufacturer may be able to help, although none of the ones I phoned could offer much advice. For guidance, here are some approximate weights:

Still wine 12 x 75cl bottles: 15kg
Champagne or Crémant 12 x (heavier) 75cl bottles: 20kg
Pack of beer 24 x 33cl bottles: 13kg (cans are lighter)
Spirits 1 litre: 2kg

If your wine is in wooden boxes, allow for an extra kilogram per case.

So if you add it all up, assuming you've bought your full champagne allowance, but that it isn't packed in wooden boxes, the total weighs around a staggering 370kg. My own experience, in a Rover, is that a dozen cases of wine in the boot and the luggage on the back seat is just about as much as you'll manage. The best thing to do is to add to the load a couple of cases at a time. The driver should soon notice when things are getting heavy. Don't forget to pump up the tyres as the load grows.

A word of warning: be extremely careful where you leave the car once you've reached the stage of storing suitcases on the back seat. To any passing thief, luggage left on seats means that the boot is probably full, too, and this is easily verifiable by pushing down on the back of the car.

If you want to bring back as much alcohol as physically possible, buying wine 'from the pump' can be advantageous. This is known as buying *en vrac*, in bulk, and it involves you bringing over a large plastic container which is filled at the cellar by a device looking exactly like a petrol pump. You buy by the litre. The finest wines won't be sold like this, of course, it's much too undignified, but often it isn't just cheap plonk; I've seen many AC wines sold this way. Apart from price – it's always cheaper than the equivalent wine in bottle – the main advantage is weight. You're not carting all that glass home.

Some people bottle the wine when they get back, which is fine if you know how to sterilize your bottles (get a home-brew buff to help). If you leave it in the container, though, beware. It's not a vacuum, and as the wine is drunk the air that takes its place will slowly turn what's left to vinegar. Best drink it all at once. If you'd like to experiment with this method, most estates which sell *en vrac* will also sell you a 5-litre plastic cubitainer, or 'cubi', for a few francs.

Even using this method, I doubt whether the average family car, holding two passengers and their luggage, will be able to exceed the new import limits. Let's be precise: it's not a limit, but simply the level below which you don't have to justify yourself. Above that, and you have to prove the wine is for your personal consumption. If you've borrowed a friend's transit van, with its larger payload, this suddenly becomes more of a problem, so make sure you've got a good reason for purchase all prepared.

Customs were full of promises that if you say the wine is for a family wedding they'll want to see an invitation. Perhaps they will. They certainly still try to look as intimidating as possible when you drive past their Customs shed (oh, how liberating it is not to see those red and green channels any more!). If you've been buying wine direct from growers, it's quite possible that you will have bought wine in two categories: for drinking now or over the next few months, and for laying down to drink in a year or two. The indicative levels are meant to be a gauge of how much wine you personally are likely to drink in a year. It's a moot point – which year are we talking about?

This guide is based on the idea that the best bargains, in both taste and price, are to be found in the château and vineyard. That doesn't mean I ignore French supermarkets on my trips, however. On the contrary. Although you won't catch me buying wine there, beer is another matter. It's amazingly cheap, and you can bring 110 litres home with you. Spirits, too, are available at duty-free price levels, so you can legally import them in far larger quantities, if your liver can stand it – 10 litres instead of just 2 on the boat.

I'll also be buying up fruit and vegetables, especially wonderful, waxy potatoes such as Ratte, Belle de Fontenay or Charlotte; salted or smoked pork called *poitrine*, not unlike bacon, either chopped or in a piece, for flavouring casseroles; tins of *cassoulet* (thick haricot bean stew), goose fat (nothing like it for fried potatoes), duck *confit*; even, if I get really carried away, tins of *haricots verts* (because the British equivalents just don't taste the same).

If I discover a market going on just before I leave, I'll do the shopping there, but don't underestimate the quality of the produce available in the hypermarkets. We entertain all sorts of romantic notions about how the French only shop at markets or in tiny specialist stores, but who do you think keeps the hypermarkets in business? It's not just down to beer-hungry Brits, the French use them as a matter of course. And demand good-quality produce, too. And get it, which is more than we often do.

A final word: let your wine rest once you've got it home. Wine is a living thing; and if you're exhausted after being bounced about in a car for 800km, so is the wine. If you open a bottle the night of your return, you're in danger of thinking you've made a major mistake. There's a good chance the wine simply won't taste right because it's all shook up. Wait three to four weeks before tasting it again.

GETTING AROUND, GETTING ALONG

DRIVING IN FRANCE

On the right, of course. Easy to say, easy to forget. Every time you start the engine, the navigator should remind the driver. You can pull off a petrol station forecourt onto a deserted road, and without thinking take the wrong side.

The main difference when driving in France is the rule of giving way to traffic joining the road from the right, *priorité à droite*. Unfortunately this is rather muddled, as the rule applies in some circumstances and not in others. Generally, if you have priority along a stretch of road you'll see a large yellow diamond with a white border. The same sign with a grey diagonal bar across it says you've lost it.

Recently the French have discovered roundabouts. Again and again you'll come across newly laid out circles indicating the local engineer has been to roundabout school and is bursting to perfect the art. You'll see them in the strangest places. French drivers are deeply mistrustful of this new-fangled idea, and approach them with extreme caution.

Almost always, traffic on the roundabout has priority, but occasionally you'll be on one and discover the hard way that joining traffic has right of way. It's just to keep you on your toes. Your Michelin atlas contains guidance on French rules of the road, including speed limits and the symbols to tell you when you have priority on the road. Just a couple of extra points: don't exceed the speed limit. <u>Don't</u>. French traffic police can extract large fines from you on the spot. They don't take plastic, and they carry guns. It can really put a damper on your holiday. If you want to stop on the open road, pull right off the highway – don't park on the side of the road. Speed limits drop by an average of 10km per hour when it's raining (in other words, when your wipers are going).

THE FRENCH WAY OF LIFE

The French way of life differs from ours in several respects which are important to the prospective wine buyer. First of all, France treats its lunch break with proper respect. It lasts two hours and is used to consume a properly-cooked three-course meal. Most properties close from 12 to 2pm, and take a dim view of the British habit of turning up at 11.55 and looking expectantly at the tasting-table. If there's one message French winegrowers want to give their esteemed British customers, it's this: have a proper lunch! We have a dreadful reputation for not respecting food, and our attitude to lunch-time compounds it. Florent Baumard of Rochefort-sur-Loire spoke for many when he said: 'We really hate to answer the phone at lunch-time, or to hear "sorry, we got lost on the way" at 1pm'.

There are a few estates which don't mind you turning up over lunch, and I've noted this in the producer listings. I do ask you to respect the opening hours given. Take the opportunity to have a decent lunch, or lay in a good stock of picnic material. Alternatively, lunch-time is a perfect time to be on the road, taking advantage of the absence of traffic. (The corollaries to this are the need to beware the maniacs driving at great speed at 12.30 because they're late for lunch, and the erratic driving at 2.30 of those whose lunch has been too liquid.)

Picnickers are well catered for in France, with plenty of well laid out picnic areas on the wine routes, or simply with lay-bys offering stunning views (Michelin maps have a symbol for viewpoints, and there's usually somewhere to park). An alfresco lunch is also a great excuse to inspect some of the splendid shops selling picnic food. Ask for the regional or house specialities. Note that food shops will close somewhere between 12 and 1pm, so plan your picnic early.

The other major cultural difference to look out for is the French system of formal politeness, *la politesse*. It is <u>essential</u> to greet people in shops with a quiet *bonjour, messieurs-dames* and say *au revoir* when you leave. Watch what the French do. They'll acknowledge each other when entering and leaving a restaurant, for instance; it's charming, but we never do it and are thought cold and impolite as a result. Whenever anyone turns their back on you, to open a door or lead the way, they'll excuse themselves with *pardon* or tell you they're going in front of you; do likewise. Saying hello to other guests as you approach the hotel pool, for instance, acknowledges their existence and makes peaceful co-use of facilities much easier than does a stone-faced pretence that there's no-one else there.

WINE RULES AND REGULATIONS

French winemaking is very heavily regulated. The contents of your glass are a product of the soil structure and microclimate (known collectively as the *terroir*), the grape variety grown, how the vine is pruned and trained, the yield (the number of litres produced per hectare of land), how and when the grapes are harvested, how the wine is made, and how long it must mature before it's released for sale. All these factors are regulated, with different rules applying in each of the wine regions you'll visit. Compare this series of regulations to the laid-back approach in the New World: there's a whole world of difference. The rules can have quite an effect upon what you might find in the cellar, so I'll describe them in some detail.

Quality levels French wine divides into three quality types. The most basic is *vin de table*, ordinary table wine, plonk. This is sold for FF5–10 a litre in plastic bottles in the hypermarket; you won't find much of it at the properties featured here. Occasionally, however, very good wine is labelled *vin de table* – usually because a wilful young winemaker has experimented with a technique not permitted in that region.

Second come the *vins de pays*. Country wines are the success story of southwest France but are less common in the north. They're a halfway house, with some regulations applying. In the Loire, 'Vin de Pays du Jardin de la France' covers wine made in the whole of the Loire Valley, and most of it is also labelled by grape variety. The term *vin de pays* is slowly replacing 'VDQS', which stood for wines from a delimited area of a superior quality. Sauvignon de St-Bris, made in Burgundy, is an eminently respectable wine which can only be called VDQS because it's not made from the white grape variety of AC burgundy, Chardonnay.

The highest category is AC or *appellation contrôlée* wine. With a few rebellious exceptions, this title covers all the best wines of France, and these are the most heavily regulated. Controlled *appellation* wines are in increasing demand in France, where the trend has been away from plonk to higher quality wine: people are drinking less, but better. In Eurospeak, these are QWPSR, quality wines produced in a specified region. The regulations aren't set in stone, but change (slowly) according to circumstances. Further ACs are still being introduced; new names are appearing around Chablis, for instance.

In practice, what does this hierarchy mean for the vineyard visitor? At the most basic buying level it's irrelevant, but if you develop an interest and get taken round by a friendly winemaker, his or her attitudes to some of these topics will tell you a lot about the wines being made.

Terroir New World winemakers used to insist that the soil a vine grew in, or the local climate, made no difference to the quality or taste of the finished product. This may largely be the case in

Australia, but I certainly don't believe it's true in France. There are any number of producers who will offer you proof in the glass of the different tastes that can come from vines growing in different parts of the vineyard.

Aspect, in this cold northern climate, is also vitally important. The most favoured vineyards face south or southwest, to take maximum advantage of the available sun. (By contrast, look at the practice of some winemakers in Provence who plant on northern slopes to avoid overcooked grapes.) Slopes are more prized than flat land; even position on the slope matters, as you can discover in Burgundy where the best vineyard sites are marked out in meticulous detail.

Grape variety With AC wines, the grape variety (or varieties) is always specified, in the regulations if not on the label, yet there is a certain amount of flexibility in their use. Some producers grow little-known local varieties which they're allowed to blend in to give a wine more colour, say, or body.

Then there's cloning, a process whereby selection is made in the vineyard of a few vines with outstanding characteristics from which plenty of cuttings are taken. Prolific vines are very popular, as you might imagine, and can improve the yield of a vineyard no end, but critics point to dangers: less biological diversity can mean, for example, that your chosen clone is particularly susceptible to a certain viral disease. Whereas with a whole vineyard of different plants only a few would die if attacked, with clones you stand the risk of losing the lot. The argument also runs that diversity makes a richer wine; more prolific vines aren't necessarily (or even probably) high in taste. Each different vine has something to offer.

Pruning and training You'll notice in the vineyard that there are many alternative ways of training vines, varying from region to region. Vines are pruned each winter, and this is when the major decision is taken on how many bunches of grapes you'll allow to grow. If you miscalculate, and too many bunches develop, you may have to go round the vineyard in June and cut some of them off. This is known as the green harvest, or *vendange verte*. These treatments have a significant bearing on the quality of the wine.

Yield In other words, how much wine is produced from a certain patch of vines, expressed as so many hectolitres per hectare ('hecto-' means 'hundred'). Very good growing conditions give higher yields. The maximum amount of wine you can produce per hectare is determined by law in each region. Better producers aim for low yields; the more juice a vine produces the more dilute it's likely to be, and the lower the yield the higher the concentration of flavour in each bunch of grapes.

Some varieties are more prolific than others, and young vines produce more than old ones. Grapes are first harvested from a vine four years after planting, but a vine needs a few more years to become mature. After that it's in its prime, until things start to go downhill around 40 (so unlike life). What an old vine lacks in vigour, however, it makes up for in quality, so although old vines won't give you a high yield they'll give you a rich one. Some producers grub up old vines the minute the decline sets in, others will cherish them and proudly put *vieilles vignes* on the label to mark out the quality. Unfortunately there's no legal definition of what constitutes old; one man's ancient could be another woman's middle age. Rémy Gresser (qv), in Alsace, reckons he's got one vineyard that was planted by his great-grandfather after the First World War, in 1919.

Harvesting and vintage In many regions, such as Champagne, the date on which the harvest may commence is decided by committee. You can't start work before the *ban de vendange*, but you can start later. There are two methods of harvesting: by hand and by machine. Harvesting machines are great big blue things that pass up the rows of vines and vibrate each individual grape off the cluster;

pickers cut each bunch off whole with secateurs. This is an important difference, as hand-picked grapes have a better chance of getting to the cellar with their skins unbroken. Broken skin means the air can get to the grape flesh, and too much exposure oxidizes the juice – not what's wanted at all. Some red wines need the stalks for extra tannin, so their grapes can't be harvested by machine. And in certain regions, again like Champagne, harvesting must be done by hand. Where both methods are permissible, their relative merits are hotly debated. During the rainy 1993 harvest, for instance, growers who were harvesting by machine were far more sanguine about being rained off for a few days than those who had to pay teams of pickers to hang around waiting.

The weather conditions throughout the year will always have an effect on what goes into the bottle. In 1993, what looked like being a brilliant year was reduced to being merely good in many places by rain during the harvest. In April 1991, frost in the Loire reduced the subsequent harvest to 20% or less of the norm. Ask growers about the latest harvest, and compare what different people tell you. It can reveal fascinating contrasts in attitude and approach.

The Loire Valley

The vast Loire river runs over 1,000km from trickling beginnings high in the Massif Central to stately, wide Atlantic estuary at Nantes. It's a region well beloved by British tourists, who come for the river views, flat cycling country and splendid châteaux. Many of the châteaux were originally built to keep meddling dowager queens and scheming mistresses at arm's length from the Paris court – far enough away to stop them meddling, not too far to be insulting. Perhaps some would still find this convenient.

The wines of the Loire are, to generalize grossly, more expensive the further inland you go. The region is best known for its white wines, but significant amounts of red and pink are made too. Muscadet, made nearest the coast, in the Pays Nantais, used to be thought of as cheap and cheerful, but bad harvests and a syndrome that could be called 'what the market will bear' have all but put paid to that notion in the UK. In the region itself, however, you can buy a good bottle for about FF20.

Following the river east, the wine region of Anjou, around the town of Angers, concentrates on the Chenin Blanc grape, known in the Loire as Pineau de la Loire, which makes little-known but splendid dry whites and excellent sweet whites – a must for lovers of dessert wines to explore. There are basic rosés and reds, too, some of which are great value.

In Saumur they concentrate on sparkling wines, stored in caves carved straight into the hillside from the white tufa clay, and in good, chewy reds from Cabernet Franc. Touraine offers more red, particularly in Chinon and Bourgueil, plus sparkling and still whites in Vouvray and Montlouis. The river now heads north, to the city of Orléans, but the wine trail heads across country to Sancerre and Pouilly-sur-Loire, where the white grape changes again, to Sauvignon Blanc. This last wine area nestles in comfortably to Chablis and the Aube, and is covered in The Golden Triangle.

For this chapter, I have divided the route into three sections to allow you to visit each for a separate long weekend or to link them together as time allows. After Touraine, it may well seem more convenient to head back to a port rather than to continue overland, but if you do want to link Touraine with Sancerre, a suitable route is described at the end of this chapter. There's more to the Loire Valley, of course, as you'd expect from a river covering such a wide area; but I think these are the areas most worth exploring to start with.

The other fact I should mention at this stage is that this guide will ignore all the blandishments of châteaux etc – well, nearly all. Much has been written elsewhere about these beautiful buildings, and it's easy to nip off the route and follow the signs to Chenonceau if that's what takes your fancy. (And, I admit, it did mine.) But it's not something I'll be concentrating on – there's too much interesting wine about. Pick your own castles and follow me on the wine route.

PLANNING THE ROUTE

This is where the crossings from the UK's south coast ports really come into their own. Whether you take a day or a night crossing depends on where you start from in the UK and whether you prefer to be bored stiff on a six-hour day crossing with the prospect of proper French food and a decent bed at the end of it, or to sleep through the crossing but be woken up at a truly ungodly hour and spend the rest of the day in a daze. I usually take a night crossing but pay for it in drowsiness the following day.

The Brittany Ferries crossing into St-Malo, however, is long enough to let you get a decent night's sleep, and you can be in Nantes by lunch-time via a quiet dual carriageway. As a bonus, the approach to the harbour is very pretty and worth braving the freezing winds on deck for. The longer crossing has not only helped the beauty sleep but brought you closer to your final destination.

For day crossings, on the other hand, the shorter the better. Both Le Havre and Caen have reasonably convenient motorway connections and are better for reaching Saumur and Tours. Cherbourg is further, and the roads aren't so good, but it's a feasible second choice for Nantes or Angers. Dieppe is reasonable too. You can pick up the motorway at Rouen, but driving through Rouen is a horrible experience; it's very badly signposted and not recommended for the first-time visitor – A-level navigation students only.

From Calais or Ostend all roads lead to Paris, I'm afraid, and the western section of the Loire seems dauntingly far. Sancerre is easier to reach from these crossings, as is Touraine, but Anjou-Saumur and the Pays Nantais will need longer than a five-day trip if you're not to see more of the inside of your car than feels comfortable.

The Loire is ideal for 'open-jaw' trips: outward on one route, back from another port served by the same company. Consider Portsmouth–St-Malo–Caen–Portsmouth with Brittany Ferries, Southampton–Cherbourg–Dieppe–Newhaven with Stena Sealink, or Portsmouth–Cherbourg–Le Havre–Portsmouth with P&O. All the ferry companies allow you to travel this way on their cheaper tickets.

The Pays Nantais

WHAT YOU'LL SEE IN THE CELLAR

Muscadet the wine is made from Muscadet the grape, also known as Melon de Bourgogne. There's also a VDQS called Gros Plant du Pays Nantais, made from the Gros Plant, which is related to the grapes used for making cognac. It's like Muscadet only less so, being even more tart and astringent. It doesn't have much going for it, except perhaps its price.

Muscadet can be subdivided between three areas of the Pays Nantais. The best is called Muscadet de Sèvre-et-Maine (from an area south-east of Nantes, which is also the biggest area). Then there's Muscadet des Coteaux de la Loire (from northeast of Nantes), and finally plain Muscadet, from an area mainly to the south of the city.

The key factor with Muscadet is the process which leaves the wine *sur lie*, on its lees. Muscadet is by nature neutral-tasting, so you can add more flavour to the wine by allowing it to rest over winter on the dead yeast cells – the lees – once fermentation is over. The wine picks up a yeasty flavour and more character, and if it's left undisturbed will retain some of the carbon dioxide produced during fermentation, giving it a lively taste. You don't fine this wine, and you don't filter it either, preferably. You handle it as little as possible to preserve the freshness and sparkle, and bottle it straight from the tank before 1 July the year after harvest. (This is a legal date that must be complied with in order to prevent the heat of summer interfering with the wine.)

An interesting quirk in Muscadet winemaking is that the fermentation/maturation tanks are set into the floor. When you enter the cellar, which is usually at ground level, very often all you see is what looks like a series of manhole covers. Beneath these are tiled or glass fibre tanks, which you may be able to look inside. This subterranean habit evolved because producers usually didn't have below-ground cellars but wanted to find cool conditions for the wine to rest on its lees. A blanket of earth seemed just the thing. You'd think that underground tanks would be impervious to disturbance from the elements, but one producer I met refuses to bottle his wine when the wind's blowing; he says it unsettles the lees and you have to wait for absolutely still conditions to make sure that no sediment is disturbed when you bottle, or you won't get a clear wine.

Like many aspects of wine production, the practice of making Muscadet *sur lie* is open to abuse. Many consumers know that the term *sur lie* means they are buying a better wine, and are prepared to pay more for it, but there is no law stating how great a surface area of wine at the bottom of a tank should be exposed to the lees. Obviously a wine matured in a tall, thin tank won't get as much exposure to the lees as wine in a shallow tank with a big bottom, if you see what I mean. The producers I recommend below, however, play fair with their *sur lie* maturation and you can taste the difference in the glass.

EXPLORING THE PAYS NANTAIS

Working along the Loire from west to east, the Muscadet region is the first to explore. In some ways it's the easiest, too, as it's compact and there's only one main style of wine to investigate. I concentrate on the area southeast of Nantes, because it produces the best wines.

The Nantes and Anjou-Saumur wine committees clubbed together in 1993 and organized a wine route that runs seamlessly through their two regions. This was clearly not an easy task – talk to the women who were instrumental in creating it, and a shadow crosses their faces as they remember all the wrangling over routes that went on. Being on a signposted wine route can make a huge difference to direct sales, and loud were the wails from bypassed producers. The Nantais signs show a bunch of grapes in green and yellow, and are enormous; the Anjou-Saumur signs have the same logo but in orange and purple, and are more modest and therefore harder to spot.

The obvious place to begin the tour is in **Nantes** itself. This city has had a bad press, but I found it reasonably straightforward to drive through and soon found L'Hôtel, a slightly faded but welcoming establishment, without a restaurant, well placed for heading out onto the wine route. I also hear good reports of the Amiral.

Staying in the middle of a big city isn't everyone's idea of fun, and I'd offer you suggestions for country stops if I could; but, curiously, although there are plenty of good restaurants on the Muscadet wine route, decent hotels are thin on the ground. You are unlikely to stay in the region more than a night or two unless you develop a passion for the local wines, so perhaps a couple of days in the city will be OK just this once.

Being so close to the coast, Nantes has seafood and fish of unparalleled freshness. I had excellent scallops at L'Océanide, an unpretentious neighbourhood restaurant with the look of a 1930s ocean liner. La Poissonnerie is a new place, close to L'Hôtel, where mountainous *plateaux de fruits de mer*, complete with whole crabs, were the order of the day. Do book; even on a freezing Tuesday night in late autumn there wasn't a spare table in sight. Drink Muscadet, of course; nowhere is wine and food as obviously complementary as here. You can practically taste the salty sea tang in the wine. (Or was I just imagining it?)

Nantes is also a useful place to organize picnic provisions. There's a fine baker, Boulangerie Chez Marie on Rue de la Fosse, and Pascal Beillevaire's cheese shop on Rue Contrescarpe, where they'll package your cheese for a picnic or to survive the rigours of the Channel crossing. There's also a brilliant chocolate shop, G Gautier-Debotte

Loire

D751

Anjou
via Route
des Bords
de Loire

N

D115 La Ville-en-Bois ▼

Le Loroux-Bottereau

NANTES *H R*

Basse-
Goulaine *R*

D105

D307

N249

D74

N149

Vertou

D756

N249

D59

Cholet

St-Fiacre-
sur-Maine ▼

Mouzillon

La Haie-
Fouassière ▼

N149

Clisson *R*

St-Crespin-
sur-Moine

Cholet

THE PAYS NANTAIS

▼ Wine producer
H Hotel
R Restaurant
See Listings
pages 73–4
for further details

0   10   20 km

(also on Rue de la Fosse), where you step back in time into a sales
room with a gilded ceiling, mirrors, cut glass, ornate panelling and
even an ottoman to sit on while you take it all in. Gifts include
chocolates filled with Muscadet and *berlingots de Nantes* (pyramid-
shaped boiled sweets) in pretty gift boxes.

To join the wine route leave Nantes heading south, following signs
for Poitiers and Bordeaux. You'll cross two bridges spanning the Ile
Beaulieu. After the second bridge turn right, off the N149, following

signs to Vertou. This is where the marked route begins, and signposted off it you'll soon see directions for the **MAISON DES VINS DE NANTES** in **La Haie-Fouassière** (on the D74).

This is a very good place to start your tour. Financed by the wine-growers' committee, it's full of enthusiastic, multilingual staff who will give you a free tasting (including one of the rare reds made in the region), sell you up to six bottles of wine and a range of tasteful souvenirs, such as a rather nice, green *sommelier*'s apron, and hand you more maps, leaflets and stickers than you know what to do with. Perched up on the hill, you have a fine view of the vineyards – a view that may well be improved if their plan to convert an old water-tower into a viewing gallery comes off.

From the Maison du Vin to the first producer is only a short hop; turn right, back onto the D74 in the direction you came, and **BONNETEAU-GUESSLIN** is signposted off to the left. Olivier Bonneteau will show you the floor vats, the *cuve souterrain*, and you'll be offered two wines: a Muscadet de Sèvre-et-Maine, light, fresh and crisp, and the Domaine de la Ferronnière, fuller-bodied and with richer fruit. It's commonly held that Muscadet needs to be drunk young – the most recent vintage for preference. Get away from the commercial products, however, and you'll discover, as I did here, that a couple of years' bottle age can do the wine more good than you'd expect.

The unassuming M Bonneteau, who speaks excellent English, says: 'I try to make Muscadet, no more no less, with all its typicity and flavour'. His prices are astonishing, ranging from FF19 to FF22.40, and represent really excellent value.

From La Haie turn back onto the wine route and head for **CHÉREAU-CARRÉ**, signposted to the right off the D59 after **St-Fiacre-sur-Maine**. (Strictly speaking this means doubling back, but I don't think Chéreau-Carré is the best place to start the tour.)

This is a large operation, comprising six separate estates, with a commercial outlook. English-speaking guides will show you the vineyards and a ruined tower complete with secret passage (inaccessible, alas, although you can climb the tower). The grounds are pretty and the cellars are decorated with grotesque woodcarvings of Rabelais characters. There's a barrel with a glass panel to show you what the lees look like.

They specialize in ageing Muscadet in oak, not something commonly done and not something I particularly warmed to, either, and you're unlikely to meet the winemaker and be able to find out why he does it. Prices here are nearly double those at Bonneteau-Guesslin, reflecting perhaps the cost of marketing activity. Do you think the wines are nearly twice as good?

If all this prickly, fresh, acidic wine has given you an appetite, then stay on the route as far as **Clisson**; it's very clearly waymarked. (If you're really feeling peckish, avoid the spur signposted off on the right to Aigrefeuille. You'll only have to turn around and come back again.) Clisson is a pretty town full of Italianate architecture with a medieval castle and covered market hall.

La Bonne Auberge is a Michelin-starred restaurant, but friendly and unpretentious, offering good value at lunch-time with a menu for FF95 upwards and an excellent selection of local wines. Smashing scallops. After lunch, stroll through the town, or leave on the N149 in the direction of Cholet and turn right into a villa where you can walk through the grounds and admire the view.

Retrace your steps and pick up the wine route again as it leaves Clisson on the St-Crespin-sur-Moine road. When you reach **Mouzillon**, look out for Xavier Gouraud's **DOMAINE DES RIGOLES DU PIN**. This is another small property run by a husband-and-wife team, and they're totally committed to their winemaking. This is where they won't bottle if it's windy. And because Mouzillon is a late-ripening area, sometimes they bottle the wine after the deadline of 30 June. That means they can't label the wine *sur lie*, but you can certainly taste the quality in the glass. Here, too, the wines give the lie to the idea that Muscadet can't age; there's an '87 for FF28, and more recent wines ranging from FF16 for the Gros Plant to FF21–25 for Muscadet.

On the first Saturday in July, Mouzillon holds a Nuit du Muscadet which looks like quite a party, judging by the photos on view in various albums in the tasting-room.

Incidentally, there's a biscuit made in Mouzillon which is often served to accompany wine tastings. Some of these are completely sugar-free, which is OK, but avoid the slightly sweet ones; they'll make the wine taste sour.

Onward again, on the route (I defy you to get lost on this one, signs are so insistent) to Le Loroux-Bottereau. Here, if you wish, deviate onto the D115 in the direction of Landemont; the **ABBAYE DE STE-RADEGONDE** is signposted on the left at **La Ville-en-Bois**. I mention this place because they've set up a rather interesting wine museum, full of old implements. There's even a travelling still in the courtyard, its bottom helpfully punched out by the French government just in case anyone gets ideas about putting it into use again. Marvel at the pain endured by the wearer of the chain-mail gloves used to strip the vine-stems of parasites.

Ah yes, the wines. Well, there's a very average Muscadet and a pleasant, light red Gamay. There's also a most peculiar-tasting sparkling wine. You may prefer to see the museum and leave a donation in the collecting-box before making your excuses.

In the tradition of leaving the best until last, here's a restaurant I'd rate as unmissable. You can catch this one at the end of a Muscadet tour, or while following the pretty Route des Bords de Loire towards Angers. Villa Mon Rêve is north of **Basse-Goulaine**, where the wine route finishes. Look out for a right turn off the D751 just after the intersection with the N249.

Chef Gérard Ryngel looks just like Pavarotti, as demonstrated by the remarkably friendly caricature of him by Ralph Steadman (drawn <u>after</u> lunch, apparently, which explains it). He shows no sign of Pavarottian temperament, however, producing instead meals of high quality featuring local produce, notably pike. Watch out for his potato purée – it's 50% butter. He didn't get where he is today by producing lean cuisine. In winter he serves *tarte Muscadet*: 'not using a tart Muscadet'. The wine list, apparently the longest in Nantes, is full of Muscadet, with prices starting at FF70. Here I drank the 1976 vintage which for me finally laid to rest the Muscadet-can't-age notion.

He has a fascinating attitude to menu pricing. In effect, all starters and all main courses cost the same. If you want to eat for a certain price, tell him, and he'll create a menu for exactly that figure with wines to match each course. In the winter, he and his wife host Sunday lunch around a huge table. If ever there was a restaurant operating from the heart, this is it.

From here it's either back to Nantes for a last night, or directly onwards to Anjou and inland to more dramatic countryside. If you're heading back into Nantes, watch out for the heavy traffic. Most people live south of the city, where it's cheaper, and the queues leaving Nantes in the evening can be horrendous.

Anjou-Saumur

WHAT YOU'LL FIND IN THE CELLAR

You'll find all styles of wine here. The white grape is now the Chenin Blanc, which is used for sparkling wines in Saumur, where its high acidity is very important, and for sweet Coteaux du Layon and the intense, dry Savennières.

Anjou Rouge is made from Gamay or Cabernets Franc and Sauvignon, and varies in quality from basic to rather good. One step up is Anjou-Villages, made exclusively from Cabernet and only in the Layon and Aubance valleys. Saumur-Champigny is often the most intense, deep-coloured of all Anjou's reds. It's currently very popular in Paris, which explains its higher price.

Anjou is closely associated with rosé wines. Fashion has turned against rosé and production is declining, but some producers, notably Didier Richou (qv), will offer you very fine pink wines without a blush.

EXPLORING ANJOU-SAUMUR

From Nantes, pick up the Route des Bords de Loire at **Basse-Goulaine** (the D751). This is well signposted and indeed forms part of the wine route connecting the Pays Nantais with Anjou, running close to the south bank. You pass first through Muscadet vineyards and those of Coteaux d'Ancenis, light red and pink VDQS wines from Gamay and Cabernet.

If your tour starts in Anjou, the town of **Angers** is a fine place to stop, once you've braced yourself to deal with big-town traffic. One of my favourite hotels in the glamorous-room/fancy food class is here, the Pavillon Le Quéré. The Le Quérés (he cooks, she organizes

20 km

10

0

SAUMUR *H R*

Parnay ▼

Chinon

D947

Varrains ▼

Les Rosiers *H R* ●

D751

St-Hilaire-St-Florent ●

D960

Doué-la-Fontaine ▼

Le Puy-
Notre-Dame ▼

D178

D178

D960

D84

D125

D167

Mozé-sur-Louet ▼

ANGERS
H R

Thouarcé ▼

D123

091N

D55

St-Lambert-
du-Lattay ▼

Rochefort-
sur-Loire ▼

D106

Savennières ▼

D751

D125

Loire

Nantes

Chaudefonds-
sur-Layon ▼

N23

Nantes

N ←

ANJOU-SAUMUR

▼ Wine producer
H Hotel
R Restaurant
See Listings
pages 74–6
for further details

front-of-house and, particularly, the wine list) opened this operation, set in a beautiful 19th century town house, only a couple of years ago, after building a reputation for fine cooking elsewhere in the town. Bedrooms are named after Anjou *appellations* and are elegant-modern in style; mine had the fanciest bathroom I've enjoyed in a long time. Food, served in a conservatory dining-room, is modern and Michelin-starred.

Leave Angers on the N23 in the direction of Nantes, turning off on the right, onto the D106, to **Savennières**. (If you're approaching from Nantes, on the D751, turn left in Rochefort-sur-Loire and cross the river to reach the village.)

Savennières is a small *appellation*, making dry Chenin Blanc whites. They used to make sweet wines here, requiring low yields. The law changed the wine from sweet to dry in 1952, but didn't increase the permitted yields to match. That means the dry whites from Savennières are very powerful, concentrated, long-lasting wines. Although many experts rate these among the greatest whites in the world, they're hardly known in the UK, and I really think it's worth getting acquainted.

Another quirk of the region is that nearly all the wines are made by women. Mme Joly started it all by buying the entire CLOS DE LA COULÉE DE SERRANT vineyard in 1959 (not as daunting as it sounds, it's only 7ha). From Savennières, follow the road to Epiré and you'll see the estate signposted off to the right. Today the wines are made by her son Nicolas, merchant banker turned advocate of biodynamic agriculture – an approach which involves working the land when the astronomical conjunctions are favourable and treating the vines with homeopathic plant sprays.

If this philosophy interests you (and it certainly does me) M Joly will offer you a passionate explanation of it. If you taste the results, you will understand why he's able to charge so much for them – the

Coulée de Serrant has the depth and intensity you would expect from such passionate commitment. This is not an estate for casual visits (there's a hefty minimum purchase price of FF300, although a range of wines more modestly priced than the Coulée is available), but for an in-depth exploration of a wine you can't do better. M Joly knows he's way out on a limb compared to current accepted thinking, but points to the fact that some of France's finest estates now grow their grapes biodynamically, so there's more to it than meets the eye – fascinating.

Do take the opportunity to walk in the vineyards, as the view from high above the river is stunning. The next estate, **DOMAINE AUX MOINES**, also has beautiful vineyard views (retrace your steps along the road to Savennières to reach it). Mme Laroche owns part of the vineyard La Roche-aux-Moines, as do the Jolys; that, and Coulée de Serrant, are the two named *crus* or growths you'll find in Savennières.

Mme Laroche is bird-like and intense. Her wines have a markedly different character in each vintage and provide an object lesson in how much wines from the same vineyard are influenced by the year's changing weather.

At both these properties you'll notice the elegant formal gardens and expansive architecture, revealing that money has been made from their vineyards for several centuries (indeed, the Roche-aux-Moines was planted by monks in the 12th century).

DOMAINE DU CLOSEL also has a fine château setting. Run by Mme de Jessey, tall and with a ready laugh, this property lies near the centre of the village on the banks of the river, and visitors are welcome to walk and picnic in the grounds.

Mme de Jessey plays a major role in promoting the wines of Savennières, lamenting the fact that the local council won't put up signs in the village to guide visitors to winemakers (something every wine explorer suffers for the lack of). In addition to classic Savennières (prices start at just FF50), Mme de Jessey offers good quality, well-priced reds.

For a picture of the younger generation of woman winemaker in action, head back over the bridge to the south bank. Stop first, if you wish, for lunch or a stroll in the pretty village of Béhuard, marooned on a narrow island in the middle of the Loire and accessible from the bridge. Then, in **Rochefort-sur-Loire**, turn left by the church and head out of the village, with the cemetery on your left. After about 800m turn right by a hut and you'll find the **MOULIN DE CHAUVIGNÉ**.

This is a brand-new estate. Sylvie Termeau and her partner Christian Plessis produced their first vintage in 1992. She's proud of the 80-year-old vines planted on her land, with their low, concentrated yields. She makes excellent Savennières, a smooth Coteaux du Layon and an Anjou Rouge.

It's difficult starting up a wine estate from scratch – vineyards are hard to find, the investment in machinery is enormous and the wine ties up your money for years while you wait for it to mature. The Moulin de Chauvigné is about as far from the grand estates north of the river as it's possible to be, but Sylvie draws inspiration from the longer-established women winemakers whose example she follows. Her wines are very fairly priced, good value for money and well worth your support, and you'll receive a friendly welcome here and as full an explanation of the wines as you desire.

Returning to Rochefort, look out for the **DOMAINE DES BAUMARD** estate on the right just after the cemetery. Here, young Florent Baumard won't show you the cellars ('no aesthetic attractions') but will take you to an 18th century tasting-room, complete with original wall-paintings, and offer a selection of the estate's range including Savennières (made for drinking much sooner than the long-lived Joly style) and the sweet Quarts de Chaume, only made around

Rochefort. (Incidentally, Anjou's other sweet wine, Bonnezeaux, is made around Thouarcé.) There's also Anjou Rouge, which I bought here in 1992 for about FF24 a bottle, and it was splendid – lean, chewy, an ideal summer red.

Newcomers to Loire wines are in safe hands at Baumard. Florent, who speaks faultless English, said: 'We don't mind people knowing nothing about wine and are very happy to help them discover new pleasures. They may help us discover their pleasures. We don't like people pretending they know about wine who are just pretenders, but we are afraid there is nothing we can do about it'.

The tour now heads away from the Loire into sweet wine territory. If you're convinced that you can't stand the stuff, please don't be put off this part of the route – the road meanders along the little River Layon, through very attractive scenery.

In the Layon Valley, autumn morning mists encourage the grapes to rot. This is 'noble rot', *Botrytis cinerea*, the same grey rot that's the scourge of British gardeners. The tiny filaments of mould pierce the grape-skin and then the heat of the afternoon sun allows the water in the grape juice to evaporate through the holes, producing a honeyed concentration in the remaining juice that's absolutely delicious. You need plenty of acidity to balance such sweetness, and Chenin has an abundance of it. These wines are little-known in the UK, and deserve closer acquaintance.

First, if you will, a little detour. From Rochefort turn right onto the D751. In Denée turn right onto the D123 and then look out for **DOMAINE RICHOU** on your right, before **Mozé-sur-Louet**. Didier Richou makes a wide range of good wines at remarkably fair prices. His sweet wine is Coteaux de l'Aubance, similar in style to Layon wines, from along the River Aubance which runs parallel to the Layon. He offers a dry Chenin Blanc called Anjou Sec for FF24, and very well rounded reds – the Anjou-Villages, from old vines, for

FF27, is the best of these. He has good rosés, too, and even a sparkler. His cellars aren't especially interesting but he has a large, welcoming tasting-room and is very hospitable.

Retrace your steps through Rochefort, along a piece of road by now becoming very familiar, and pick up the wine road on the left where it turns off the D751. This takes you onto one of the prettiest sections of the route, and to one of the finest producers you'll meet in these pages.

DOMAINE GAUDARD is on the wine route at **Chaudefonds-sur-Layon**. Pierre Aguilas doesn't speak English, but says it doesn't matter a jot and that communication is never a problem with his British visitors. Hardly surprising in a man with such enthusiasm for his product.

He offers various Coteaux du Layon from different villages, showing incredible concentration, most notably the Cuvée Claire, named after the woman who runs the local wine committee. I'm not usually one to rave about the tropical fruit salad tastes I find in my glass but I'm afraid it's unavoidable here. More prosaic, but also good, is the firm red Anjou-Villages.

This is an ideal place to come if you want the very best of the sweet wines of the region and to find out more about the subtle differences in flavour between various villages' wines. There's plenty of room to taste, with tables and stools, informative displays and outdoor seating in summer. One to raise the spirits.

The wine route now leads you into **St-Lambert-du-Lattay**. It's worth stopping here for the splendid **MUSÉE DE LA VIGNE ET DU VIN**, which I think is just about the best I've come across. Much more than simply displays of old implements, the exhibits give a real sense of the movement of work with the seasons and the weather. It doesn't take itself too seriously, either – look out for a series of rude wine-related pictures hidden behind screens, which you have to tug a cord to reveal. There's a game to play involving pulling out drawers full of wine-type smells, and even a tasting-fountain which is filled with Coteaux du Layon on special occasions. Next door a Maison du Vin offers tastings of local wines.

In St-Lambert turn off the wine route onto the N160, heading southwest, and you'll soon see the **DOMAINE DU SAUVEROY** on your right, looking like a ranch house. Pascal Cailleau, not yet 30, runs the estate with skill and overwhelming enthusiasm. He offers a wide range of well-priced wines: rosé FF19.50, Anjou-Villages FF23, Coteaux du Layon FF23 upwards, sparkler FF36. He'll also sell you wines from the pump for ridiculously little. Ask him to point you towards a walk in his vineyards, high above the valley floor.

Now let us take an overview, briefly. For some reason, decent country hotels are hard to find in this region. It's perfectly possible to travel from Nantes to Saumur in a day, if you're linking the two regions, but you won't have much time for vineyard visiting and a first night in Angers is well worth considering (the town also has plenty of architectural and historical interest). But you might prefer instead to be based in Saumur and make a couple of circular trips. Saumur is a lovely place to stay in, which is why I'm mentioning it now rather than waiting until it comes along in the normal course of things.

To continue: head back into St-Lambert to rejoin the wine route, the D55 and then the D125. (Watch out for the narrow bends in St-Lambert. I was staggered by the size of the juggernauts that force their way through the tiny town, and they don't take prisoners.) The wine road meanders through pretty countryside with plenty of picnic opportunities.

After **Thouarcé**, look out for a sign on the left to the **CHÂTEAU DE FESLES**. It's a beautiful building, in fine, well-kept grounds. One of France's most famous *pâtissiers*, Gaston Lenotre, is part owner and his image is much in evidence (Quentin Crisp fans will admire his hat), as is his influence, in sugar and chocolate sculptures, displays of local breads, and the inevitable books for sale.

Make an appointment with an English-speaking guide and you'll enter an air-conditioned room full of barrels bought after one year's use from top sweet winemakers Château d'Yquem. See the fermentation cellars, full of stainless steel tanks and controlled by a wonderful electronic console looking exactly like an early computerized theatre lighting board. You can see this console through a glass partition in the tasting-room. Digital read-outs reveal the precise temperature each vat is fermenting at, and you can input new temperatures at will (which is exactly what my guide did. No doubt the cellar-master cursed him). Code: green light = chiller on, red light = heater on. There's also an enormous *tri* table. Every bunch of grapes brought in passes across this table at harvest and is sorted by hand according to quality.

Note the horse's head above the entrance, denoting that the building was formerly stables. Prices are higher than the norm here but the Anjou Rouge, for instance, although FF32, has won several awards and is gorgeous. And if you buy 11 bottles you get a twelfth one free. Is this an offer you can't refuse?

Onward now to Saumur, either following the wine road or, for the impatient, heading for Doué-la-Fontaine and taking the D960 direct to town. Staying on the wine route has the advantage of bringing you into **Le Puy-Notre-Dame**, along the D178, where you'll find the **Château de Beauregard** if you're lucky (or, like me, phone them from outside the 13th century church after 15 minutes' fruitless searching and they'll come and find you).

Mme Gourdon will show you round the charming, small estate and into the cellar tasting-room. They've only been bottling their own wine since 1989, when her husband took over from his father;

previously they sold all the wine to the local co-op. Their Cabernet de Saumur Rosé is bottled in sterilized bottles with an absolute minimum of carbon dioxide: 'So no headache'. Hangover-proof wine must be the coming thing. This is a very attractive wine, as is their Saumur Rouge and, for that matter, their Saumur Blanc. There's one sweetish (*moelleux*) wine for FF50 and all the others sell for FF25, which must make book-keeping easy.

The Gourdons don't get many visitors yet, and would like more, so you should receive a warm welcome. They also have a very imaginative way of disposing of the bottles they open for tasting...

There are two hotels I'd recommend in **Saumur**, but neither has a restaurant so you can ring the changes each night; plenty of good places to eat at are within reach. The hotel with the best view is the Anne d'Anjou, restored from ruin a decade or so ago. It faces the Loire and I think the best rooms are those with a river view. There's a splendid staircase with a *trompe-l'oeil* ceiling, and parking at the back. The staff are enormously helpful. To reach it, carry on along the main street even when it appears to be for pedestrians only, and turn right at an improbably tiny roundabout on the banks of the river. It's on the right just after a second roundabout.

Cheaper, but no less considerately-staffed, is the Central (from the main street into town turn left just as the road becomes 'pedestrian priority', then sharp right into a tiny side-street). All the rooms are differently decorated and there's a subterranean car park.

The Central has the advantage of being right by what I mentally named Restaurant Street, Rue St-Nicolas. All manner of food is here, plus an excellent picnic shop, Le Traiteur, great for cheese, salads and *rillettes* (potted meats). I enjoyed the cooking at Les Chandelles. Two other reasonably-priced options are near each other on the Rue Maréchal Leclerc, the main road out of town but within easy walking distance of the hotels: L'Escargot and La Croquière.

I also found some very good, simple food in a most unlikely place, the Brasserie Napoléon on the Place de la Bilange, near the tourist information centre. This is a basic bar-brasserie, with banquettes that reminded me of the coffee-bars of my adolescence. I discovered it while recovering from food poisoning, having been told to eat only vegetables. Here, surrounded by the youth of Saumur hunched over a coke, and accompanied by ZZ Top, I had splendid soup and fresh *crudités*, while my husband Ian was surprised by the best grilled lamb chops he'd been offered in a long time. Which just goes to prove the old adage that you can't judge a French eatery by its external appearance.

Saumur is a lively little town with plenty of atmosphere, dominated by the Château de Saumur perched high above it and by the Loire itself. There's a wide mix of architectural styles, particularly between the castle and the river on the tiny twisting streets of the old town (plenty of restaurants here, too). Stroll along the river-bank, it's beautiful at night with the lights beneath the bridge playing on the water.

Saumur makes a good base for touring, and you can easily make the route circular by returning to the Loire at Gennes. Across the river from Gennes, at **Les Rosiers**, the Jeanne de Laval hotel-restaurant is popular with British visitors but manages to keep a high standard of cooking nevertheless.

The town is famous for its cavalry school, the Cadre Noir, and for mushrooms (there's a museum, naturally) which grow in the damp tufa-clay cellars quarried out of the local hillsides. These caves are also crucial to the development of Saumur's famous sparkling wine, providing the constant temperature necessary while wines mature. The founder of local firm Gratien & Meyer (qv) didn't even carve out his own cellars, he simply bought up the land surrounding already-quarried caves – caves that nobody wanted; the price was correspondingly low.

Loire sparkling wines can be pink and even red as well as white. There are various *appellations*, principally Saumur and the more stringent Crémant de Loire. Still reds are made as Saumur, from Cabernets Sauvignon or Franc, or as classier Saumur-Champigny, from nine villages southeast of the town.

Several large sparkling-wine houses have their headquarters here, making a big play for visitors. I can thoroughly recommend visiting Gratien & Meyer and Bouvet-Ladubay. **BOUVET-LADUBAY** is located in **St-Hilaire-St-Florent**, just north of Saumur. A guided tour in English costs FF5, and includes the cellars and the process for making traditional method sparkling wine (see Champagne pages 124–8). Note the old packing hall, with its ornate cast-iron pillars, now used to display a collection of old carriages. Up an awkward spiral staircase there's a library of 6,000 old labels housed on revolving wooden filing cabinets. Very Victorian. It's not included on the general tour, but do ask to see it anyway.

The tour fee includes a tasting, and the wines are of very high quality, with sparklers from FF45 to FF80 and still reds from FF26 to FF39. Across the road the company has opened a museum of modern art, with a recently-renovated old theatre on the first floor.

Just along from Bouvet is **LANGLOIS-CHÂTEAU**. I wasn't so impressed by their wines but I thoroughly enjoyed the walk up into their vineyards which forms part of their longer guided tour. Take your camera: there's a splendid view of the river and across to the château.

GRATIEN & MEYER is on the other side of Saumur. As you head out along the D947 towards Chinon, their imposing buildings are set into the hillside on your right. Tours are free, in English and preceded by a 12-minute video. You'll see a section of their 10km of caves during the half-hour walk – including the Grand Caveau, a subterranean banqueting room – and all parts of the sparkling wine process, before tasting the finished product (also free).

You can take the tasting a stage further by joining one of the English-language classes at Gratien & Meyer's wine school. These cover sparkling wine production and professional tasting technique, moving on to an overview of wines from the whole of the Loire. They cost from FF35 to FF175, run from May to October and need to be booked in advance.

In sharp contrast to the shy style of sister establishment Alfred Gratien (qv) in Epernay, the visitor reception here is highly-organized and professional, but the winemaking is equally meticulous and the quality very high. Cuvée Flamme, in particular, is excellent and one of the best examples of sparkling Saumur wine.

The wine road now moves towards the heart of red Loire wine-making, Chinon and Bourgueil. Turning right from Gratien & Meyer, the road hugs the river as you pass through the Saumur-Champigny wine district (along the D947). Here there are several producers to visit. Perched high up on the hill in **Parnay** is **CHÂTEAU DE TARGÉ**. Come for the view, at least; the selection of wine could well be limited to one vintage, which may or may not be to your taste.

One other producer nearby whom I feel is worth noting is **DOMAINE DES ROCHES-NEUVES** at **Varrains**. The excellent wines made here were the hit of the Loire stand at the Decanter Wine Fair in 1993.

I mentioned the food poisoning episode (and the restaurant I suspect of guilt in this matter doesn't appear in this guide). I consulted a doctor in Saumur. You know you're in a winemaking area when the doctor doesn't warn you off alcohol but apologizes instead that your furred tongue will wreck your tasting ability. Naturally he had a hot tip, and here it is: Saumur reds to keep, in a traditional style, from Patrick Vadé at the **DOMAINE ST-VINCENT** in Saumur. Any good? No idea. I couldn't taste a thing that day.

Touraine

WHAT YOU'LL SEE IN THE CELLAR

Touraine is home to the Loire's finest reds: Chinon, Bourgueil and St-Nicolas-de-Bourgueil. These are made from Cabernet Franc, cousin of Cabernet Sauvignon (which is also permitted in small quantities). Known locally as Breton, Cabernet Franc often tastes slightly minty and 'stalky' and is leaner and less overwhelmingly blackcurranty than Sauvignon. The Loire way with red wines is not to aim for a strong, oaky taste, and the number and newness of the barrels you see in the cellar are a fair indication of the producer's attitude to this tradition.

East of Tours, the less fashionable, good-value wines include Gamay de Touraine (light, fruity red) and Sauvignon de Touraine. Sauvignon Blanc makes crisp, dry, high-acidity wines with a grassy, gooseberry taste and smell, best drunk young; the examples here are cheaper than those made in Sancerre and Pouilly-sur-Loire. Chenin Blanc is found, too, most famously in Vouvray. This grape is so malleable that you can produce dry, sweet or sparkling Vouvray, so it pays to read the label. You'll also come across some rosé.

EXPLORING TOURAINE

The easiest way of exploring Touraine is to split it down the middle, taking Tours itself as the dividing line. The division into wine regions along the Loire is fairly arbitrary as far as the wine tourist is concerned. We've moved district, to the area controlled by the city of Tours, but in reality Chinon and Bourgueil can just as easily be visited from Saumur, barely half an hour's drive away, as by decamping into the region itself. Any excuse to stay a little longer in Saumur is welcome, and I think the standard of hotels is better there, too.

If you've been following the red wine trail through Saumur–Champigny, keep going along the D947 to Montsoreau and then take the D751 following the River Vienne to Chinon. You'll notice that the *route du vin* signs have stopped; Touraine is still in the process of devising its route, aiming to have it in place by the summer of 1995.

Chinon is dominated by the ruins of its imposing castle on the skyline above the town, and its narrow old streets run beneath. Just off the main square you'll find one of the strangest wine museums around: it's animated. Accompanied by taped commentary, available in English, life-size puppets act out various processes of winemaking and cooperage from the last century. Halfway through the visit you'll be offered a tasting of Chinon wine (and jam made from the wine, as well). Usually when wine is offered for sale at a venue like this I don't barge it with a touchpole, reasoning that if the wine needs a gimmick like this to help sales it can't be good enough for people to want it in its own right. But this time I was proved wrong completely. The wine at the **MUSÉE ANIMÉ DU VIN ET DE LA TONNELLERIE** comes from one of the best producers in Chinon, **BERNARD BAUDRY**, and you can visit his cellars a few miles outside to taste in more tranquillity.

Baudry's estate is in **Sonnay**, just before Cravant-les-Coteaux on the D21, right next door to his brothers Jean and Christophe. The visit begins with a tour of the cellars, hewn out of the slope, then you can taste in the cellar, or in the small, comfortable tasting-room if it's cold.

Chinon is simply Chinon – there are no fancy Premiers Crus – but M Baudry subdivides his wine into three. There's Les Granges, from young vines, Domaine, from older vines, matured in stainless steel, and Grezeaux, matured in *barriques* (small oak barrels), plus an elegant, wood-fermented rosé. This is concentrated Chinon of excellent quality, and one of the three styles (at least) should be to your taste. Prices are fair, too, from FF23 for pink to FF35 for oaked red.

A couple of kilometres on the other side of **Cravant-les-Coteaux** you'll find the **DOMAINE DANIEL CHAUVEAU**, known as Pallus. Daniel's son Christophe is the current winemaker and both he and his wife Jemma speak excellent English. His preferences lie with using a mixture of oak and stainless steel to mature the wine. Like most of the Loire, the Chauveau estate suffered badly in the frosts of 1991, which left them with a very pale red wine, almost impossible to sell – until people began to drink it with food. Now it's very popular in Paris bistros as a wine light enough to have with lunch. My favourite vintage at Chauveau was their most recent, the '93, which was full of concentrated flavour, but it hadn't yet been filtered and I hope it's as full afterwards.

In more and more cellars, you taste the wine in cask, express admiration, then buy the same wine once it has been bottled and find all the heart has been taken out by excessive filtration. This often happens when the winemaker employs someone to filter and bottle the wine using portable equipment, a common practice if the estate is too small for it to be worth investing in the machinery yourself.

Returning to Chinon, make a circuit by turning left in Cravant and taking the riverside road back (the D8). I may be doing the town a disservice in complaining about its hotels, since whenever I've been there it's been the dead of winter, when half of them are shut. The Chinon is on the opposite bank in a kind of industrial park; there are lovely views of the castle but it's a long walk from the old town and the hotel is geared to business travellers rather than tourists. Ignore its restaurant. The Diderot is in traditional-creaky style and in just about every British guidebook. Locals speak well of the Gar'Hôtel and the Hostellerie Gargantua (the latter has a restaurant), and of L'Océanic, offering fish and seafood. You could, however, just as easily use Saumur as a base for touring the area.

Leave Chinon along the Vienne's north bank on the D749 to **Bourgueil**. This isn't a particularly scenic road, but when I reached north of Bourgueil and headed out into the vines, the slope reminded me of the Côte d'Or in Burgundy, and I warmed to it accordingly.

The two producers I'd recommend here make red wines of very good quality, on a small scale; neither speaks English. The first is **YANNICK AMIRAULT**, and his estate is signposted to the north off the D10 above Bourgueil. His little house is surrounded by vines, with the cellars a few metres down the road.

He'll show you the cellars on request and offer you both Bourgueil and its neighbouring wine St-Nicolas-de-Bourgueil. He practises *pigeage*, the Burgundian technique of plunging down the cap of grape-skins into the fermenting must. As his brochure proves, he does it by hand, or rather foot – standing in the vat, grape juice up to his shorts. He says it's worth the pain for the extra intensity in the wine. Prices range from FF31 to FF40.

PIERRE-JACQUES DRUET is based in **Benais**, east of Bourgueil. It isn't easy to get an appointment with him, and even harder to find him (I had to phone and he came to meet me). His cellars are set in old caves outside the village. He uses very low yields and oak casks to produce a wine of enormous structure and concentration which outlives its neighbours. This is definitely an advanced-student visit, an education for fans of the wines of this area who want to know how far you can push winemaking techniques before you reach the limit. Press a coin into the cellar ceiling as a memento; the salt deposits will hold it firm until you return.

From here you can return to Saumur along the edge of the wine slopes on the D10, heading back to the Loire on the D85 and then along the N152. Perhaps take a walk on the gentle vineyard slopes first – there are plenty of paths, but no waymarked routes, so follow your nose.

To move on along the Touraine tour, however, you have to pass **Tours** itself. Since it's unavoidable you may as well turn the traverse to your advantage. Tours has a very attractive old town, a cathedral and various museums, and the hotel I'd recommend, the Royal, is easy to find as it's on the main north–south route through the city. It has modern rooms of fair size and a secure underground car park.

From the Royal, walking to the main sights is easy, and there are several restaurants in the old town, all close to each other so you can poke your nose in the windows, examine the menus and see which suits you best. (Details are given on Listings page 77.)

Leave Tours on the N152, on the north bank of the Loire and you'll find **Vouvray** a few kilometres outside, signposted on the left. If, however, you'd like to continue along the route by avoiding Tours altogether, here's how: join the D751 Chinon–Tours road, and at Joué-lès-Tours follow signs for the motorway to Blois and Orléans. Join the A10 – this stretch is toll-free – and then leave it immediately

TOURS
H R

A10

Blois &
Orléans

Vouvray
H R

Cher

Loire

N152

N152 H R

TOURAINE

▼ Wine producer
H Hotel
R Restaurant
See Listings
pages 76–7
for further details

0

10

20 km

D1

Limeray
▼

Montrichard

D139

D62

D17

D114

Chaumont-
sur-Loire

Cher

Marcuil-
sur-Cher
▼

St-Aignan

St-Romain-
sur-Cher
H R

D675

Vierzon

N

after you've crossed the second bridge, at Rochecorbon. (This exit is brand new.) Now join the N152 in the direction of Blois, and Vouvray is close by.

There's a restaurant here worth stopping at, called Le Grand Vatel. The dining-room is high-ceilinged, the walls covered with murals depicting people eating, drinking and having a good time through several centuries. The excellent food includes regional specialities such as *beuchelle à la tourangelle* (veal kidneys and sweetbreads in mustard sauce with mushrooms). Half a dozen rooms in creaky-traditional style are available on half-board terms only.

Usually I avoid *demi-pension* like the plague, because I'm always afraid I'll be forced onto a menu I don't fancy, but with this one the rest of the *carte* is accessible by paying supplements. It represents value for money overall, so I'd make an exception here. The staff are very friendly, too. The village also boasts one of France's finest *charcuteries*, Hardouin, located on the main street.

Vouvray is famous for white wines, all made from Chenin Blanc and demonstrating what a versatile grape this is, producing a range from bone dry to semi-sweet and very sweet via sparkling. There are several big names in the village, but I suggest you visit one of the young rising stars instead. **DIDIER CHAMPALOU**'s small estate is high above Vouvray (take a left turn in the village, signposted Caves de la Bonne Dame, and keep going following signs for Le Grand Ormeau; the estate is signposted in a field on your left). You'll be led into a lovely, damp, musty 300-year-old cellar to taste a dry (*tendre*), a *demi-sec* or medium-dry and a sparkler made at lower pressure than most. Try this one if bubbles usually get up your nose. Try, too, the Champalous' ripe, luscious *moelleux* (mellow) wines. Prices are reasonable for the quality, which is high (sparkler FF37, *demi-sec* FF40, *moelleux* FF60–75). Catherine Champalou offers a warm welcome; she speaks good English and is delighted to explain the region's wines to you.

Wines similar to Vouvray, but less well known and therefore cheaper, are made in Montlouis. Although close as the crow flies, Montlouis is on the opposite bank of the river and involves a detour back into Tours or up to Amboise to find a bridge. It will be interesting to see what the new Touraine wine route does with this little problem.

From Vouvray you have a choice of routes to the next stop, in **Limeray**, and both are scenic. Take either the D1, which is signposted as a *route touristique*, or the main N152 down by the banks of the Loire. Entering Limeray take the left fork up the hill and **DOMAINE DUTERTRE** is on the right. Here you've moved away from the well-known *appellations*. Local wines are called Touraine-Amboise or just plain Touraine, and because these are little known, prices are lower.

Dutertre's cellars stretch into the rocks; they have a small museum displaying the firm's old implements, and a tasting-room warmed by a log fire in winter. They make reds, mainly from Cabernet Franc although they do also offer a Gamay; avoid the rosé. The whites are mostly Chenin Blanc, plus Crémant de Loire and Sauvignon de Touraine. The prices? Still wines range from FF20 to FF27, sweet wines are FF46 and Crémant is FF42; *en vrac* wines are available for even less. You can tell you've entered an unfashionable area.

From Limeray join the N152 towards Onzain and cross the river to Chaumont-sur-Loire. Take the D114, which becomes the D139 and then the D62, to reach the River Cher. Cross the river at Montrichard and follow a pretty route (the D17) along the south bank to **Mareuil-sur-Cher**. Just after the village, in the *lieu-dit* of La Méchinière, is **DOMAINE DE LA RENAUDIE**.

Patricia and Bruno Denis are the fourth generation to work this family property and make wines of extremely high quality which age well. They offer three red grape varieties: Gamay, Cabernet and the local speciality, Cot (the 't' isn't pronounced here, unlike further south). There's also a blend of these three in a wine called Tradition. These wines are not perhaps in traditional Touraine style but the results are, I think, very good indeed.

The domaine has made a big investment in new cellars and equipment over the last couple of years. There are no romantic rock-hewn caves but Patricia, who speaks excellent English and brims with enthusiasm and knowledge, will talk you through the processes, pour the wines and explain all you want to know. They sell by the litre (FF6–12) and carry a range of empty containers for sale – the largest, 33 litres, costs FF42.50. The Touraine Tradition costs FF20 a bottle and the Cabernet is FF21–28, according to age. Here is some of the best winemaking in the area and a real bargain.

Another bargain is a night's stop at Le St-Romain, at **St-Romain-sur-Cher**. (From Mareuil, head east along the D17, cross the river at St-Aignan and take the D675; the hotel is on the right in the village.) The food here is extremely good value: four excellent courses for FF62, including a dessert selection where everything is made in-house – which is most unusual at this price. Rooms cost about FF150 and for that price are clean and very entertaining, eg hand-held shower and no curtain. Bet you can't flood the floor as thoroughly as I did. The double bed was saggy, so book a twin.

If your tour ends here, join the motorway at Blois. For Sancerre, follow the Cher to Vierzon, then the D56 to St-Martin-d'Auxigny. This, I admit, is a dull town, and Menetou-Salon (take the D59 from St-Martin) is little better, but things liven up at Morogues. From there keep on the D59 until you join the road into Sancerre.

Listings

When telephoning France from the UK, the number must be preceded by the digits 010 33. Producers are listed in wine route order, and hotels/restaurants by town or village according to the route. Accommodation prices are per room, meal prices are per head.

THE PAYS NANTAIS

Producers

Maison des Vins de Nantes
Bellevue, 44690 La Haie-Fouassière
Tel 40 36 90 10
Open June–Sept Mon–Sun 8.30–12.30,
13.30–18.30; Oct–May Mon–Fri to 18.00
Credit cards accepted
Good English

Bonneteau-Guesslin
Domaine de la Juiverie,
44690 La Haie-Fouassière
Tel 40 54 80 38
Open Mon–Sat 9–12.30, 14–18;
closed during harvest
Good English

Chéreau-Carré
Château de Chasseloir,
44690 St-Fiacre-sur-Maine
Tel 40 54 81 15
Open Mon–Sat 8–18 incl lunch-time;
visits by appointment Sun
Credit cards accepted
Some English

Domaine des Rigoles du Pin
44330 Mouzillon
Tel 40 36 62 85
Visits by appointment Mon–Sat 9–12,
14.30–18.30; closed Feb & 1–15 Aug
Some English

Abbaye de Ste-Radegonde
44430 Le Loroux-Bottereau
Tel 40 03 74 78
Open Mon–Fri 9–12, 14–17;
visits by appointment
Sat & Sun
Some English (by appointment)

Hotels and Restaurants
H Hotel *R* Restaurant

Nantes

H Amiral
26 rue Scribe, 44000 Nantes
Tel 40 69 20 21, Fax 40 73 98 13
FF269–319

H L'Hôtel
6 rue Henry IV, 44000 Nantes
Tel 40 29 30 31, Fax 40 29 00 95
FF360–400

R L'Océanide
2 rue Paul Bellamy
(Place du Pont Morand)
Tel 40 20 32 28
FF94–260

R La Poissonnerie
4 rue Léon Maitre
Tel 40 47 79 50
Plateaux de fruits de mer FF90/150/220

Clisson
R La Bonne Auberge
1 rue Olivier de Clisson
Tel 40 54 01 90
FF95–280

Basse-Goulaine
R Villa Mon Rêve
Route des Bords de Loire
Tel 40 03 55 50
FF156–320 (or ad lib)

ANJOU-SAUMUR

Producers
Clos de la Coulée de Serrant
Château de la Roche-aux-Moines,
49170 Savennières
Tel 41 72 22 32, Fax 41 72 28 68
Open Mon–Sat 8–12, 14–18
(minimum purchase price FF300
for a tasting)
Credit cards accepted
Good English

Domaine Aux Moines
49170 Savennières
Tel 41 72 21 33, Fax 41 88 59 12
Open Mon–Sat 9.30–12, 14–17;
visits by appointment Sun
(minimum purchase 3 bottles)
Credit cards accepted
Good English

Domaine du Closel
1 place du Mail
49170 Savennières
Tel 41 72 81 00, Fax 41 72 86 00
Open Mon–Sat 9–12.30, 13.30–18,
Sun 9–12.30
(minimum purchase 3 bottles)
Credit cards accepted
Good English

Moulin de Chauvigné
49190 Rochefort-sur-Loire
Tel 41 78 86 56
Open Mon–Sun 9–19 'except lunch';
appointment preferred
Good English

Domaine des Baumard
49190 Rochefort-sur-Loire
Tel 41 78 70 03, Fax 41 78 83 82
Visits by appointment Mon–Fri
10–12, 14–18
Sterling accepted
Good English (from Florent & Isabelle)

Domaine Richou
Chauvigné, 49610 Mozé-sur-Louet
Tel 41 78 72 13, Fax 41 78 76 05
Open Mon–Sat 8.30–12, 14.15–19
(minimum purchase 6 bottles preferred)
Good English

Domaine Gaudard
La Brosse, 49290 Chaudefonds-sur-Layon
Tel 41 78 10 68, Fax 41 78 67 72
Open Mon–Sat 9–12, 14–19; visits by
appointment Sun; closed Sun in winter
Credit cards accepted
English: '3 words'

Musée de la Vigne et du Vin
Place des Vignerons,
49750 St-Lambert-du-Lattay
Tel 41 78 41 48
Open April–Oct

Domaine du Sauveroy
49750 St-Lambert-du-Lattay
Tel 41 78 30 59, Fax 41 78 46 43
Open June–Sept Tues–Sat 9–12, 14–19;
visits by appointment Oct–May and
all year Sun & Mon
Credit cards accepted
Good English

Château de Fesles
49380 Thouarcé
Tel 41 54 14 32, Fax 41 54 06 10
Open Mon–Sat 9–18 incl lunch-time;
visits by appointment Sun
Credit cards accepted
Good English (by appointment)

Château de Beauregard
4 rue St-Julien,
49260 Le Puy-Notre-Dame
Tel 41 52 24 46, Fax 41 52 39 96
Visits by appointment Mon–Sun
(minimum purchase 6 bottles,
3 if sweet)
Some English

Bouvet-Ladubay
1 rue de l'Abbaye,
49400 St-Hilaire-St-Florent
Tel 41 50 11 12, Fax 41 50 24 32
Open Mon–Sun 8–12.30, 14–18;
April–Sept incl lunch-time
(admission FF5)
Credit cards accepted
Good English (on request)

Langlois-Château
3 rue Léopold-Palustre,
49426 St-Hilaire-St-Florent
Tel 41 50 28 14, Fax 41 50 26 29
Open Mon–Sun 10–12.30, 14–18.30;
closed Jan; closed Nov, Dec, Feb,
March on Mon & Tues (tours FF5–18;
the 2-hour FF18 tour is by appointment
or on Thurs at 10.00)
Credit cards accepted
Tours in English (on request)

Gratien & Meyer
Route de Montsoreau, 49401 Saumur
Tel 41 51 01 54, Fax 41 51 03 55
Open March–Oct Mon–Sun 9–11.30,
14–17.30; Nov–Feb Mon–Fri 9–11.15,

14–17.15, Sat & Sun 10–11.45, 15–17.15
Good English
(For information on wine courses held
at Château Gratien contact Catherine
Gohier on the above number or Alfred
Gratien (qv) in Epernay.)

Château de Targé
49730 Parnay
Tel 41 38 11 50, Fax 41 38 16 19
Open Mon–Sat 8–12, 14–18;
closes Sat at 16.00
Credit cards accepted
Good English (by appointment
with M Pisani-Ferry)

Domaine des Roches-Neuves
56 boulevard St-Vincent,
49400 Varrains
Tel 41 52 94 02, Fax 41 52 49 30
Visits by appointment
Good English

Domaine St-Vincent
49400 Saumur
Tel 41 67 43 19
Visits by appointment
No English

Hotels and Restaurants
H Hotel   **R** Restaurant

Angers
HR Pavillon Le Quéré
3 boulevard Maréchal Foch,
49000 Angers
Tel 41 20 00 20, Fax 41 20 06 20
Rooms FF500–800, Meals FF220–450

H St-Julien
9 place Ralliement, 49000 Angers
Tel 41 88 41 62, Fax 41 20 95 19
FF230–320

R La Rose d'Or
21 rue Delaâge
Tel 41 88 38 38
FF100–170

Saumur
H Anne d'Anjou
32 quai Mayaud, 49400 Saumur
Tel 41 67 22 42, Fax 41 67 51 00
FF260–640
(There is a fancy restaurant in the
garden, Les Ménestrels.)

H Central
23 rue Daillé, 49400 Saumur
Tel 41 51 05 78, Fax 41 67 82 35
FF210–310

R Brasserie Napoléon
Place de la Bilange
FF60–120

R Les Chandelles
71 rue St-Nicolas
Tel 41 67 20 40
FF120–290

R La Croquière
42 rue Maréchal Leclerc
Tel 41 51 31 45
FF70–157

R L'Escargot
30 rue Maréchal Leclerc
Tel 41 51 20 88
FF73–115

Les Rosiers
HR Jean de Laval
Route Nationale, 49350 Les Rosiers
Tel 41 51 80 17, Fax 41 38 04 18
Rooms FF350–650, Meals FF180–420

TOURAINE

Producers
Musée Animé du Vin
    et de la Tonnellerie
12 rue Voltaire, 37500 Chinon
Open summer Mon–Sun
10–12.30, 14–19
(25-minute tour; admission FF23)
English commentary

Bernard Baudry
13 Coteau de Sonnay,
37500 Cravant-les-Coteaux
Tel 47 93 15 79, Fax 47 98 44 44
Visits by appointment Mon–Sat 9–12,
14–18; closed end Aug & early Sept
Some English

Domaine Daniel Chauveau, Pallus
37500 Cravant-les-Coteaux
Tel 47 93 06 12, Fax 47 93 93 06
Open Mon–Sat 8–12.30, 14–18.30;
appointment preferred, essential for Sun
Credit cards accepted
Good English

Yannick Amirault
La Coudraye, 37140 Bourgueil
Tel 47 97 78 07, Fax 47 97 94 78
Open Mon–Sat 8–19 incl lunch-time;
appointment preferred
No English

Pierre-Jacques Druet
Le Pied-Fourrier, 37140 Benais
Tel 47 97 37 34
Visits by appointment
Credit cards accepted
No English

Catherine & Didier Champalou
Le Portail, 7 rue du Grand Ormeau,
37210 Vouvray
Tel 47 52 64 49, Fax 47 52 67 99
Open Mon–Sat 9–12, 14–18;

appointment preferred, essential for Sun
Good English

Domaine Dutertre
Place du Tertre, 20–21 rue d'Enfer,
Limeray, 37530 Amboise
Tel 47 30 10 69, Fax 47 30 06 92
Open Mon–Sat 9–12, 14–18;
visits by appointment Sun
Credit cards accepted
Some English

Domaine de la Renaudie
La Méchinière, 41110 Mareuil-sur-Cher
Tel 54 75 18 72, Fax 54 75 27 65
Open Mon–Sat 'all day incl lunch-time';
visits by appointment Sun; closed last
week Aug
Good English

Hotels and Restaurants
H Hotel   **R** Restaurant

Chinon
HR Hostellerie Gargantua
73 rue Haute-St-Maurice,
37500 Chinon
Tel 47 93 04 71
Rooms FF240–600, Meals FF150–200

H Le Chinon
Centre St-Jacques, 37500 Chinon
Tel 47 98 46 46, Fax 47 98 35 44
FF310–380

H Diderot
4 rue Buffon, 37500 Chinon
Tel 47 93 18 87, Fax 47 93 37 10
FF225–380

H Gar'Hôtel
14 avenue Gambetta, 37500 Chinon
Tel 47 93 00 86, Fax 47 93 36 38
FF210–240

R L'Océanic
13 rue Rabelais
Tel 47 93 44 55
FF98–145

Tours
H Le Royal
65 avenue Grammont, 37000 Tours
Tel 47 64 71 78, Fax 47 05 84 62
FF335–398

Old town restaurants:
R La Galette des Rois
Place Plumereau
Tel 47 05 77 17
FF150

R La Poivrière
13 rue Change
Tel 47 20 85 41
FF95–260

R Le Relais des Cigognes
Place Plumereau
Tel 47 20 57 57
FF145

R Zafferano
47 rue Grand-Marché
Tel 47 38 90 77
FF85–150

Vouvray
HR Le Grand Vatel
Avenue Brûlée, 37210 Vouvray
Tel 47 52 70 32, Fax 47 52 74 52
Rooms FF200–260, Meals FF125–220,
half board, FF400–460 for two

HR Le St-Romain
41140 St-Romain-sur-Cher
Tel 54 71 71 10, Fax 54 71 72 89
Rooms FF142–152, Meals FF62–198

Burgundy

Burgundy wines are some of the most expensive in the world. And some of them are worth the money, while others trade emptily on their name. Yet there are bargains, or at least better value wines, to be had if you know where to look. This chapter will do three things: explain why these wines are so expensive, describe a route that takes you through some of the world's most evocative wine names, and tell you who to call on to buy well-made wines at fair prices.

Winemaking in Burgundy goes back to the Greeks, the Romans or the early years AD, depending on who you believe. It was built up by the Church, with several monastic orders establishing major vineyard holdings, and by the State in the form of the Dukes of Burgundy. These dukes controlled most of northern France and the Low Countries, and were great patrons of the arts, which is one of the reasons Burgundy is so rich in art treasures today.

The French Revolution wiped out the land ownership of both church and aristocracy, splitting up the huge vineyard holdings. Then the Napoleonic Code decreed that on death a man's landholdings be split equally among all his sons. Small vineyards became smaller still with each succeeding generation, creating today's crazy patchwork of tiny holdings. The often quoted example is that of the Clos de Vougeot vineyard, covering 50ha and owned by about 80 people. No wonder you can't rely on the name of the vineyard to guarantee good wine.

Burgundy wines come from five regions: Chablis, the Côte d'Or, the Côte Chalonnaise, the Mâconnais and Beaujolais. This chapter deals only with the Côte d'Or and Côte Chalonnaise. The Chablis wine route is described in The Golden Triangle, but the Mâconnais and Beaujolais are rather too far to travel for an extended weekend. (Another book perhaps...) Added to which, Beaujolais wine is made from a different grape (Gamay) and is completely different in style from other burgundies; in many ways it is best grouped with the wines of the Rhône.

The Côte d'Or, or Golden Slope, is the heart of great Burgundy winemaking. It is also tiny. From just south of Dijon it runs a mere 50km down to its southern border at Santenay. The region pivots around Beaune, roughly its centre. From just north of Beaune up to the suburbs of Dijon is the Côte de Nuits, while Beaune itself and south to Santenay is known as the Côte de Beaune. Stretching above these two regions, higher up the slopes, are the Hautes Côtes de Nuits and the Hautes Côtes de Beaune. The Côte d'Or is a narrow outcrop of rock, and grapes are grown all along its side and on the valley floor beneath, but the best wines come from a slim strip that runs along the slope roughly halfway down.

Wine production on the Côte d'Or and neighbouring Côte Chalonnaise totals about a fifth of the amount produced in rival region Bordeaux. So one of the main reasons burgundy is so expensive is simple supply and demand. We want more of it than they've got. And they know it, which is the second reason it's so expensive – a case of 'charging what the market will bear' again. Luckily the market is currently proving that it won't bear so much, and prices are slipping back from their late 1980s heights.

The third reason is that the red grape of burgundy, Pinot Noir, is extremely difficult to grow. It's sensitive to frost, to rot, to over-production... you name it, it's offended by it. The cost of preventative measures is high and this in turn adds to the price you pay.

When everything goes well, however, Burgundy's Pinots outclass the rest of the world's. So there's really no competition: burgundy is the best and you have to pay accordingly. Not surprisingly, about three-quarters of the Côte d'Or is planted with Pinot Noir, leaving less and less room for the great white burgundy grape, Chardonnay. Now this one is easy to grow, so there are no cost problems here – but the problem lies in scarcity value. Supply and demand come into play again. Everybody wants the rich, unctuous white wines of Burgundy and of course there are not enough to go round.

However, where Santenay ends, the Côte Chalonnaise begins, running for perhaps 25km as far south as Buxy. Worldwide demand for these wines is less intense, and if anywhere can be said to represent good value in Burgundy winemaking, it is here.

WHO MAKES THE WINE?

Because of the way land has been divided and subdivided there are thousands of winemakers in Burgundy and, ooh, dozens of them are making really good wine. Most of the producers I suggest you visit grow their own grapes and make and bottle their own wine, but not all. The *négociant*, or merchant, has had a huge role to play in shaping Burgundy's recent fortunes and influencing what the wines taste like.

The *négociants* were powerful at the end of the last century, when a louse called *Phylloxera vastatrix* (because its destruction was so vast) laid waste to nearly all Europe's vineyards. This plague destroyed many livelihoods. By the time they discovered how to graft the old vines onto phylloxera-resistant American rootstocks many producers had gone out of business. Gradually the vineyards were replanted, but young vines don't produce grapes with much oomph, and the resulting wines were pale and watery. The merchants began to import wines from the south, from the Midi, and especially from French Algeria, to blend with the feeble burgundy and add colour and body.

This practice spread, and continued long after the newly-planted vines had reached maturity. It became the dominant winemaking style for Burgundy reds, so much so that today, long after this adulteration has been banned and (for the most part) stopped, there's a generation of wine-lovers, not least in the UK, who sigh softly in remembrance of the deep red, thick, alcoholic, robust burgundy of yesteryear. Never mind that it was an impostor, that's the way it was when they grew to love it, and they want it back. The growers described below, however, will show you light, elegant wines of great finesse, and I hope you'll like them. I have included in my suggestions a couple of *négociants* of very differing styles, as examples of what they have to offer and of the benefits and problems you might encounter when buying wines from the *négoce*.

Négociants operate in several ways: they can buy grapes from the grower, or buy the fermented young wine in cask and keep it while it matures (known as *élevage* – literally 'upbringing'). Selling to a *négociant* has many advantages for the grower, not the least of which is cash upfront. No tedious waiting around while the wine matures in cask and then in bottle; the money is in within months of the harvest (it's almost as good as making Beaujolais Nouveau). If you grow grapes on many different parcels of land, all needing to be vinified separately, the *négociant*'s economies of scale make a great deal of sense. Unfortunately *négociants*' wines can taste more like all the other wines they produce than like other wines made from that village or vineyard.

On the other hand, retailers and restaurants want to buy wines in sufficiently large quantities to ensure continuity of supply. They want their customers to build up 'relationships' with the wines sold. A few hundred cases per year is no use to them, thank you very much. And if you know the names of good, reliable *négociants*, such as Latour, Jadot or Drouhin, it helps when you're desperately scanning a restaurant's wine list or searching along a wine merchant's shelf for a name you can trust.

In Burgundy, perhaps more than anywhere else in France, you need to be able to trust the producer's name. The source of the wine – the vineyard – is not enough. Take the Clos de Vougeot again: it may be a Grand Cru, but, alas, this fact is not nearly enough to guarantee that what's in your glass will be worth the inordinate price you paid for it. The equation has to be 'site' plus 'producer' equals 'worth buying'.

Vintage plays a part, too. It's certainly true to say that a good producer will make good wines in a bad year, but the effect of the vintage will have some bearing on the keeping qualities of the wine, and on how long you have to wait before it's ready to drink. Luckily there's been a succession of good vintages since 1987 (which was written off as a bad year only because it was bad in Bordeaux).

HOW THE WINES ARE CLASSIFIED

The ladder of classification in Burgundy moves from the general, covering the whole region, to the specific, covering only one named vineyard. Nearly all the wines in Burgundy are *appellation contrôlée*, or AC, meaning they are made to specific regulations.

The broadest classes, the regional, reveal little about the wine. The most basic reds are Bourgogne Grand Ordinaire (probably made from Gamay, more ordinary than grand, ho ho) and Bourgogne Passetoutgrains, which is at least one-third Pinot Noir. The safest place to start is with Bourgogne Rouge, which is usually 100% Pinot Noir. Even the greatest estates often produce a little generic burgundy, and you'll frequently find that a plain Bourgogne Rouge from someone good is better than a fancier label from someone you've never heard of.

For the basic whites, Bourgogne Blanc must be 100% Chardonnay or Pinot Blanc. Although no-one shouts about it, a fair amount of Pinot Blanc is grown in these parts. A lively alternative is Bourgogne

Aligoté. The Aligoté at its best makes crisp, fresh, fruity wines and is the classic base wine for making Kir (although whatever you do, don't tell the top Aligoté producers that you intend to adulterate their lovely wine in this way).

Kir is the Burgundy aperitif, made with *crème de cassis* from locally-produced blackcurrants. A sparkling version, Kir Royale, is made with Crémant de Bourgogne. Crémant is another generic *appellation*, for sparkling wine made in the same way as champagne, in other words by second fermentation in bottle. I find these very good value indeed, at half the price of a bottle of champagne.

The above classes of wine apply to the whole of Burgundy. Some regional *appellations*, however, are more specific, applying just to one part. The Hautes Côtes de Beaune and Hautes Côtes de Nuits *appellations* offer red and white wines made from grapes grown above the main Golden Slope. Then there is the little Côte de Beaune area, just outside Beaune, and the village of Bouzeron in the Côte Chalonnaise which is allowed to attach its name to the production of Aligoté. The *appellations* Côte de Beaune-Villages and Côte de Nuits-Villages cover wines from the less important villages on one or other half of the Côte d'Or. (The name of the village may be added as a suffix.)

Now things become much more specific. The next level up is called *village* or AC *communale*. Here you put only the name of your village or commune on the label. If you wish, you can also show the name of the specific vineyard the wine came from but, if you do, the name must be in smaller letters. This may seem pedantic, but it's supposed to prevent the consumer from confusing these wines with the top two quality levels, Premier Cru and Grand Cru.

Premier Cru wines have the name of the village and the name of the vineyard on the label, usually in letters the same height. Sometimes the grower streamlines the issue by putting only these two pieces of information on as a title, but if so you'll always find the words 'Premier Cru' somewhere on the label to reassure you that this isn't simply a *village* wine masquerading as something better.

Top of the pecking order, the Grand Cru wines disdain to tell you what village they're from; here all you get on the label is the name of the vineyard. The words 'Grand Cru' will also appear somewhere, if in smaller print. Incidentally 'Grand Cru' is not to be confused with 'Grand Vin de Bourgogne', which many growers put on their labels. 'Grand Cru' is a legally-controlled designation; 'Grand Vin', or 'great wine', is simply the grower's opinion.

Certain villages have annexed the name of their most famous Grand Cru vineyard onto the village name, for promotional purposes. Aloxe hyphenated Corton, its best vineyard, onto its name; Puligny and Chassagne both claimed Montrachet; Gevrey added Chambertin. This causes confusion because you also have Grand Cru vineyards with hyphenated names. Chambertin is a Grand Cru vineyard, for instance. So, too, is Charmes–Chambertin. But the words 'Gevrey-Chambertin' on a label simply indicate a *village* wine. Hyphenation alone is no guide to what is a *village* wine and what is a Grand Cru. If you intend to move in these rarefied circles you need to know which is which.

WHAT YOU'LL SEE IN THE CELLAR

Burgundy has much to offer the cellar visitor because of the different techniques growers practise. As the domaines are often very small, you're unlikely to be confronted with rows of gleaming stainless steel towers. Things are done on a small scale, often by hand, often in wood.

In particular, there are many variants on the Burgundian technique of *pigeage*. The aim of this process is to draw more red colour out of the thin-skinned Pinot Noir grape. The grapes are crushed, and perhaps destemmed, and put into open vats skins and all. When fermentation starts, the vigorous bubbling sends the skins floating to the top of the vat where they form a cap, which is not much use since you need the skins to circulate in the vat to give off more colour. Twice a day, therefore, the cap of skins and stalks is pushed back down into the wine.

There are many ways of doing this: the traditional method was to use the feet while standing in the vat and clinging onto the sides for dear life. This is still the method on many estates, but it's dangerous because of the carbon dioxide given off during fermentation. Three men were reported to have died this way during the 1993 harvest on the Côte d'Or.

Alternatively, you can use a plunger that looks like the thing you unblock drains with on a long pole, or even a tree branch with a cluster of little stumpy branch fingers left on the end. I used one of these to push the cap down in Irancy, near Chablis, and found it surprisingly hard work; the cap offers a lot of resistance. Then there are mechanical aids – pneumatically- or mechanically-operated cap-busters suspended on ceiling tracks that you can move by motor. These require a large investment of money and a strong ceiling, and are worth looking out for – particularly when in action.

Once fermentation is over, the wines, whether red or white, are put into vats or barrels to mature. The creamy-vanilla taste given by new oak is highly prized in burgundy, in both whites and reds, and the general principal is, the finer the wine the more new oak barrels are used. Some growers use new barrels, old barrels and even stainless steel vats, in different proportions depending on the quality of the vintage and the wine, and assemble a blend of the wines before bottling.

Listen out while you're in Burgundy for strains of a huge winemaking controversy fomented by a Lebanese oenologist, or wine scientist, Guy Accad. He's encouraging makers of red wine to turn their usual methods upside down. It's generally thought necessary to heat the grape juice, or must, in order to get it to fermentation temperature as quickly as possible. A high temperature encourages the colour in the grape-skins out into the wine. Accad's theory demands the reverse of this. He says that the grapes should be left at a cool temperature to macerate before fermentation begins – a method which results in really deeply-coloured grape juice. Opponents of this approach say the resulting wine doesn't taste like proper burgundy, and they liken it more to the darker, spicier reds of the Rhône. Proponents say that when the wine is mature it will be classic burgundy. It's still a little early to know for certain which is true, but it's worth being aware of this violent diversity of technique and opinion before you visit a Burgundian cellar.

PLANNING THE ROUTE

Getting to Burgundy is easiest via Calais or Ostend/Zeebrugge. From Calais the journey along the recently opened motorway from Reims to Dijon via Troyes takes about 6 hours (605km). This is a splendid road. It's much quieter than the route via Paris, and a bird-watcher's delight: birds of prey dot the route, sitting on fence posts. I counted over twenty on a recent quiet Sunday.

From Ostend, the route is via Brussels and Luxembourg, dropping down to Burgundy via Metz, and allows you to take advantage of a great deal of free motorway. The toll from Calais to Reims is FF86, and from Reims to Beaune FF113, but there are no tolls in Belgium or Luxembourg, and Metz to Nancy is, unusually, also a toll-free stretch.

One of the joys of travelling in Burgundy is its compactness. This gives you several options. You can move on every night, often with only short distances to travel between hotels; you can base yourself in Beaune, following a different wine route each day; or you can pick three centres as you move south. If taking the last option, I'd suggest Gevrey-Chambertin for the Côte de Nuits, Beaune for the Côte de Beaune, and one of a selection of villages for the Côte Chalonnaise (see pages 108–9). The principal hotel recommendations for the first two stopping places have no restaurant, which I think is better for a multi-night stay as you can try a different place each night, all helpfully within walking distance. The Côte Chalonnaise hotels have restaurants, all offering genuine Burgundian cooking at different levels of price and finesse.

Burgundian food is usually described as 'hearty'; take this to mean large pieces of meat in rich, unctuous sauces, strange combinations (such as eggs in red wine – I've tried it three times and still can't abide it) and huge quantities. A Burgundian starter is a normal person's main course. Watch out especially for their salads. A 'peasant's salad' may sound innocuous, but it's a trap: a little bit of lettuce arrives crushed beneath the weight of a heap of croûtons and bacon lardons, perhaps even with a poached egg on top. Don't get me wrong; it's really tasty. It's also all I wanted for lunch, but several other equally gargantuan courses followed it. I know this sounds like a complaint, but it's not meant to be one, it's just that since I got back my clothes don't fit like they used to.

Naturally a region so well regarded for its cuisine will produce plenty of good picnic food. If eating outdoors is your thing, head for the hills. There are plenty of pretty spots for vineyard picnics, but the views from the wine routes high up in the Hautes Côtes are stunning. In particular look out for the one high above St-Romain.

I don't offer a producer recommendation for every village. There wouldn't be room to discuss them all, for one thing, and producers often own parcels in several communes. Some, indeed, have property from one end of the Côte d'Or to the other. But between them, the producers listed below will be able to sell you wines from nearly every *appellation*.

They'll also sell you a bottle of wine for about FF40, and some for FF30 or less. No-one recommended will lure you in and then show you nothing but wine at FF200 a bottle. Even if some offer the finest wines from the Côte, with prices pitched accordingly, you should always be able to find others at lower prices – no unpleasant surprises.

There are several *routes du vin* signposted (I use the term loosely) on the Côte d'Or. You'll see signs for the Route des Grands Crus and various sets of markers in the Hautes Côtes; in the Côte Chalonnaise you'll occasionally see old, blue enamel *route du vin* signs. Don't worry if these signs disappear at vital crossroads; the region is so compact that you have to work quite hard to get lost.

The routes I describe don't always follow the official ones. I chose them because I like them and because they link together well. It's easy to use them as a base and then to strike out on your own and just follow your nose. The vineyard roads are very pretty but not always passable by car. Sometimes they peter out into dirt tracks (I was caught out in this way in the hills above Mercurey) and become better walking or cycling territory. I keep promising myself that one day I'll go to Burgundy without dashing from producer to producer and just cycle sedately among the vines. One day...

EXPLORING THE CÔTE D'OR

I suggest leaving the motorway at Nuits-St-Georges, itself an important wine town, and heading north up the main N74 to the first base village, **Gevrey-Chambertin**. If you've taken an early ferry (say at about 8am) from Dover, or an overnight into Ostend/ Zeebrugge, it'll be early evening and all you'll probably want to do is get to the hotel and collapse. If you've had a fair distance to travel before hitting the Channel ports, I suggest breaking your journey in Champagne, at one of the hotels recommended in that section. (Several of them are near the motorway: see pages 130–2.)

BURGUNDY

▼ Wine producer
H Hotel
R Restaurant
See Listings pages 113–6
for further details

A good base in Gevrey is Les Grands Crus, a modern hotel in the heart of the vineyards, within sight of the cellars belonging to the first producer to visit. All the restaurants I'd recommend are within walking distance. At Le Petit Caveau you'll find cheap Burgundian cooking, while the Bonbistrot has attractive, rustic décor and a short menu of regional dishes. Then there's La Sommellerie, mid-range in price, modern in style and with a warm welcome; and top of the range is Les Millésimes, a very fine table.

As an alternative, a five-minute car journey brings you north to **Fixin**, where the Relais de l'Empereur hides really hearty, peasant dishes and pleasant service behind an unpromising exterior (don't be put off, go to the side entrance).

Gevrey-Chambertin is, for me, where the Côte de Nuits starts to get interesting. This is where the great red wine Grands and Premiers Crus vineyards begin to appear. The most famous Grand Cru here is the Chambertin, and all the others have tacked its name onto theirs to confer additional prestige. Only one, however, Chambertin Clos de Bèze, was deemed sufficiently good to use Chambertin as a prefix; all the others have to add the glamour name as a suffix, such as Charmes-Chambertin. Incidentally, you can drive past the Chambertin vineyard on the D122; there are large signs at either end proclaiming: 'Ici commence Le Chambertin'. They make a splendid photo-opportunity against a backdrop of vines and, I hope, blue sky.

DOMAINE DENIS MORTET is in the heart of the village. M Mortet has invested heavily in building a new bottle cellar and tasting-area, where he receives visitors. He doesn't speak English but his wife does; between them they explained a philosophy very much bound up with the soil and simplicity. 'We've got exceptional *terroir* here in Gevrey-Chambertin and it behoves us to do the best we possibly can with its products'. This entails rigorously selecting the grapes you make wine with, throwing out any underripe or rotten ones (known as the *tri*) and keeping yields low for better concentration. He doesn't filter, which he believes removes too much matter from the wine and reduces its concentration. All he does is use egg white to fine the wine, which he says doesn't fatigue it and gives it brilliance. Simple, eh? What I want to know is what happens to all the egg yolks. Perhaps that explains the local popularity of *crème brûlée*.

Truly, the proof of the pudding is in the glass, and you can buy some exceedingly well made wines here. He'll sell you generic burgundy such as an Aligoté for FF28 and a basic Bourgogne Rouge, which has very good colour and concentration, for FF42.

His '92 Premiers and Grands Crus weren't yet bottled when I tasted them but he made an assembly of each from different casks, just as he would on a larger scale in a few weeks' time when he came to bottle. I was really impressed by the intensity of these wines and the sheer pleasure of tasting them. They'll certainly keep but they were surprisingly enjoyable for ones so young. His top prices range from FF128 for the Premiers Crus to a whopping FF259 for the Chambertin Grand Cru. This is indeed the price league you're in when buying the best that Burgundy has to offer, but bear in mind that you'll probably pay double these prices in the UK. I think Domaine Mortet is a splendid place to begin burgundy investigations.

Leaving Gevrey-Chambertin on the D122, signposted the Route des Grands Crus, you're soon out in the vineyards and the scenery is lovely: you're passing through some of the world's most valuable agricultural land. (The photo-opportunity is coming up on your right.)

Morey-St-Denis, a little-known and underrated village in the shadow of more famous neighbours, is close by. Here you may like to visit **DOMAINE DUJAC**. Run by Jacques Seysses and his Californian wife Ros, this is one of the finest and most influential estates in Burgundy. It was set up by Seysses in the late 1960s (Dujac = du Jacques) and makes wines that are elegant and complex, yet similar in price to very inferior burgundy sold elsewhere.

Here's the 'oak equation' in action: he uses 100% new oak barrels for the Grand Cru wines, 50% for the Premiers Crus. It's not as expensive as it sounds, Ros explained, because you can sell the barrels on after you've used them, for half what you paid. So if she paid FF2,000 for a new barrel and can get FF1,000 for it a few years later, she's happy.

Visiting Dujac is strictly by appointment: 'Otherwise the welcome is less than welcoming', as Ros put it. Dujac is also interesting for the connoisseur of red tape. Wine is sold in France with a green *capsule congé* stuck on the top of the bottle, which indicates that tax has been paid and it's authorized for sale. Ros doesn't use these capsules. Her view is that since most of their wine is exported it's too much like hard work putting them on and then having to take them off again if the wine is to be sent abroad.

Instead, she goes down to the local tax official in the village and has the documentation completed for each wine sale to private customers. You might think it was fiddly and time-consuming but Ros doesn't seem to mind. What she usually asks you to do is come back and collect your order the next day. Meanwhile she'll prepare the paperwork and also label and pack your bottles. (Most properties only label enough bottles for their immediate needs. Wine needs to be stored in nice damp cellars, damp enough to peel the labels off in days. It's better to do it on demand.) You'll get a fancy document showing details such as your licence plate and how many hours you'll be travelling with the wine, in an attempt to stop fraudulent double journeys with the same paperwork.

You are likely here to be invited into the cellar to taste the new vintage from cask. Then you can ask to taste one or two wines from the current list. Many Dujac customers return year after year, buying in bottle what they tasted in cask a couple of years before, but the Dujacs only have about five British private customers: 'whom we welcome with open arms'. This estate deserves to be much better known among wine explorers. The *village* wines cost FF112–118 for the Morey-St-Denis, depending on the vintage, and FF100–106 for the Chambolle-Musigny. Premiers Crus approach FF200 a bottle, Grands Crus up to FF250. These are really delicious wines, well worth your attention. There are no generic reds, but there's Aligoté for FF42 and Bourgogne Chardonnay for FF60.

The road now leads to Chambolle-Musigny, passing the Grands Crus vineyards Bonnes Mares and Clos de Tart on your right. From Chambolle, head for the Clos de Vougeot, just above **Vougeot** itself and visible from quite a distance.

The Clos de Vougeot is an essential visit, both for its historical interest and for the role it plays today in promoting Burgundy wine. The vineyard was originally planted by Cistercian monks in the 13th and 14th centuries. Then they built the wall around it and finally the buildings known as the **CHÂTEAU DU CLOS DE VOUGEOT**. Both vineyards and château were sold off after the French Revolution and the château was eventually bought in 1944 by the Confrérie des Chevaliers du Tastevin (roughly: The Brotherhood of the Knights of the Wine-Tasting-Cup). This brotherhood was formed a decade earlier to promote the wines of Burgundy, and was and is extremely successful. The members hold massive 500-guest dinners at the château several times a year and initiate new Knights, who have to dress up in cod medieval red robes and get through the ceremony without giggling. A visit to the château involves a guided tour (in English by request) including several amazing old wine presses and a slide show full of pictures of other people enjoying themselves at the Brotherhood banquets. Cost FF15, duration about 45 minutes.

The Knights have no connection with the vineyard, they own only the château. After the vineyards were sold off in 1789, ownership gradually became more and more fragmented, until today when there are about 80 owners (I'm vague because the figure keeps changing as parcels are bought and sold). Eighty people divided into

50ha results in an average annual production of less than 2,500 bottles each, although obviously some own more land than others. A number of these 80 make their own wine, others sell their grapes to *négociants* and yet others farm their land out under sharecropping arrangements. This chequer-board of ownership is a microcosm of the problems you have in trying to buy a decent bottle of burgundy anywhere in the region, or indeed in any UK high street. How can you rely on knowing the names of the good vineyards? It's not enough. You also need to know the names of good producers.

One of the best in Clos de Vougeot is **CHÂTEAU DE LA TOUR**, and happily it's very well geared up to receiving visitors. It's the only estate situated within the walls of the Clos making and maturing its wines actually on site. Turn right on leaving Château du Clos, and it's about 100m down the road. During the season – Easter to November – English-speaking staff are on hand, but out of season you can be seen by appointment (which also gives you a chance to ring their splendid bell, with an old hunk of vine as a bell-pull). You taste in a first-floor room with a splendid view of the vineyard. Ask to see the cellars, too.

The family-owned property has 5ha in the Clos de Vougeot and also other vineyards, but the other sites' wines, although on sale here, are marketed under different names. In the last century, family ancestors were *négociants* in Beaune. They owned part of the Clos vineyards and stored the wines at the Château du Clos. In 1891, however, the château was sold and the family had to remove its stocks. Rather than transport 150,000 bottles by horse to Beaune they decided to build a storage cellar within the Clos (the roots of the present property) and then built a little railway to transport the bottles there.

Château de la Tour's Clos-Vougeot wine ranges from FF180 to FF260, depending on the vintage, and it's delicious. (I know, at that price wine should be, but so often in Burgundy it isn't.) The château also offers generics from FF30 and a Crémant for FF40, so you don't have to break the bank in order to visit.

Vougeot itself need not detain you. If you're in need of a hearty lunch, drop down onto the N74 and cross over to **Flagey-Echézeaux**. There's a bistro here called Robert Losset, rustic in appearance and heavy on the cream. It's hearty, popular and cheap.

Alternatively, loop back up Vougeot's one-way system (by turning left in the village and left again) and continue past the Château du Clos, and the Echézeaux and Grands Echézeaux vineyards, into **Vosne-Romanée**. If you want to pay homage, head high out of the village to the Romanée-Conti and other Romanée vineyards – the dearest in all Burgundy. And I do mean dear. How does £700 a bottle (from a UK wine merchant) strike you?

To set foot more firmly in reality, join the main N74 in the direction of Beaune, and you'll soon see **DOMAINE ARMELLE & BERNARD RION** on your left. This young couple has established a formidable reputation but the wines are as yet relatively unknown and thus better value. Armelle speaks enough English to talk about the estate and its wines, and will guide you through the cellars to a small, cosy tasting-area.

Their generic wines are all of very good quality and at fair prices – FF20 for Grand Ordinaire, FF25 for Aligoté, FF40 for Bourgogne Rouge. They have a range of Grands and Premiers Crus, all very well made and keenly priced, and they also have that rarity, a selection of bottles from older vintages. I know of no better treat than the present of a bottle of wine from a significant vintage (although I did take the precaution of getting married in the bumper year of 1985).

Now you're practically on the outskirts of **Nuits-St-Georges**. Although this is the home of many important figures in the wine world, and its architecture betrays that there has been a lot of money here for many centuries, I don't find it as interesting as what lies just down the road. So if you're staying another night in Gevrey-Chambertin, head back via the D25 (turn right on the northern outskirts of Nuits; the road is signposted – just once – Route des Hautes Côtes). This is a pretty road, through some of the Hautes Côtes vineyards. After about 3km bear right on the D35, and then right again onto the D31 after Semezanges, and descend via the steep, pretty Combe de Lavaux into Gevrey. Incidentally, this road takes you past La Gentilhommière, a very quiet hotel with motel-style rooms, heated swimming-pool and popular restaurant. Alternatively, stop in Nuits if you will, and then head out again on the N74 towards Beaune (I do hope they've finished their interminable roadworks by the time you read this).

The next producer on the route is just south of Nuits, at **Premeaux-Prissey**. Turn off left at the church, and 100m down the road you'll see **DOMAINE BERTRAND AMBROISE** on the left. I really enjoyed my visit here. M Ambroise speaks good English and is a genial host, happy to explain his wines and his philosophy. His tasting-cellar is long on atmosphere, with a wood-fired stove blazing in winter. Generations of grape-pickers have covered the beams with chalked graffiti.

The wines are full and round and have lots to offer. His generic red is a snip at FF32 and he offers a range of smashing wines from various Premiers Crus, including Nuits-St-Georges, Gevrey-Chambertin and Monthélie. He also has the white Grand Cru Corton-Charlemagne, and it is gorgeous. M Ambroise doesn't get many visitors, only about a hundred a year, because: 'Everybody just speeds through on the main road'. Do stop. It's worth it.

Now the N74 heads through some fairly dull scenery, past the industrial areas surrounding Comblanchien and Corgoloin, mainly devoted to quarrying. Here we pass the border between the Côte de Nuits and the Côte de Beaune, and the main road has nothing whatsoever to commend it. You can turn off left onto the D20F at Corgoloin, through Ladoix-Serrigny towards the next stop, Chorey-lès-Beaune.

The small village of **Chorey-lès-Beaune** is often ignored; there are no top vineyards here, not even any slopes. Yet the two growers I'd recommend both make wines at *village* level which are very good value and will be ready to drink much sooner than the wines at sky-high prices. The first, **TOLLOT-BEAUT** (I can't resist sounding all the 't's in a robust northern English accent), is a small family firm run by three brothers and their three children, who plan by taking collective decisions at daily meetings. Nathalie Tollot is in charge of sales. Her English is excellent and she'll take you – by appointment – into the cellars to taste a well-made range of wines. Their main production is of *village* wine from Chorey itself and surrounding villages, although they have very fairly priced generics, some Premier Cru reds, and red and white Grand Cru from Corton.

Tollot-Beaut was one of the first properties to bottle its wines on the estate for shipment to the American market, back in the 1920s when most producers were still shipping in cask. Consequently, it's well geared up to exporting and the wines are widely available in the UK, but not all that widely known, probably because production is concentrated in the mid-priced range. I've been buying wine here for several years and have always been impressed. It's good stuff.

The second domaine to visit, that of **JACQUES GERMAIN**, is located in the Château de Chorey (to find it, just look up; it's the tallest building in town). Here you can taste some very well made, elegant wines in the old cellars (there's another splendid bell to ring if nobody's around) and take the opportunity to walk through the formal park and grounds.

The domaine also offers elegant, expensive bed and breakfast. The setting is very attractive but there are no restaurants in the village and you either have to drive into Beaune or take pot luck with the restaurants on the N74. To me, that's a disadvantage, as I don't like to drive after dinner, although it's no problem for those with a teetotaller in the party (but if you are one, why are you reading this book?).

Now head out of Chorey and cross the N74 to the pretty village of
Savigny-lès-Beaune. You can taste Savigny reds at Tollot-Beaut
(qv), or the splendid, rare white Savigny at Château de la Tour (qv).
Leave via the D2, heading north; you'll pass a simple Logis,
L'Ouvrée, which has its own cellars (and hence a very fairly priced
wine list). The road winds along the side of a lovely wooded valley
to **Bouilland**, where there's a temple of gastronomy, Le Vieux
Moulin, with well-situated rooms in the annexe opposite.

After Bouilland turn right onto the D18 and the road descends back
into Hautes Côtes territory and to **Pernand-Vergelesses**. This is
another unappreciated Burgundy village, possibly because of the
dangers of pronouncing the name wrongly in restaurants.

Turn off the D18 into **Aloxe-Corton** – the road first takes you past
the white Grand Cru vineyard Corton-Charlemagne, followed by
the beginning of the various parts of the Grand Cru Corton vineyard. The architecture is attractive, with several châteaux and the
ornate, mosaic-tiled Burgundy roofs. The area also offers ideal
walking territory, into the hills around the Grand Cru vineyards.
Finally, rejoin the N74 and head into Beaune.

Beaune is a very special place for me. Never mind that it's full of
tourists during the season. I love stopping here and always manage
to find an excuse to travel via the town no matter where in France
I'm headed for.

It's a medieval city, built by the Dukes of Burgundy before they
moved north to Dijon, and is still surrounded by ramparts; the one-
way ring-road circles them, traffic moving anticlockwise. Entering
from Dijon, you are confronted as you join the ring-road by the
impressive, arched Porte St-Nicolas. Halfway round the ring-road
you'll find both the hotels I'd recommend. The Hôtel de la Poste is
just before the turning off to Chagny on the N74, the Hostellerie de
la Bretonnière is 100m down that turning, on the left.

The Poste is a grand, old-fashioned establishment; I can imagine it as a coaching-inn. It's recently been refurbished and has an elegant piano-bar with something of the air of a 1930s liner (although the pianist is electronic, courtesy of Yamaha). The restaurant serves traditional, expensive food. Although I enjoyed eating here, it's also convenient to treat the Poste as a base for exploring some of the excellent restaurants within the ramparts.

The Bretonnière, on the other hand, is modern and without a restaurant; it's an easy walk from here to the town centre. Rooms vary in price; the simplest is FF175 but the ones I prefer are the newest, costing about FF350, set motel-style in a second courtyard at the back. Both hotels offer off-street parking; Beaune is compact, and by far the best way to explore it is on foot.

Top of my current restaurant list is Le Jardin des Remparts for modern, innovative cooking, full of flavour, marred only by rather arrogant young staff. La Ciboulette offers good-value, simple cooking in charming surroundings, and well-chosen, fairly-priced wines. There's also a relatively hip wine bar, Le Bistrot Bourguignon, which has a good selection of wines by the glass and simple *plats*, perfect for a light lunch. The Central hotel – also a decent place to stay – has a restaurant that's well spoken of. Good picnic shops are near at hand on the pedestrianized streets off Place Carnot. All these are within the ramparts.

The key wine-tourist visit is the Hôtel-Dieu. This was founded in 1443 by Nicolas Rolin, chancellor to one of the Dukes of Burgundy, who bequeathed all his possessions to endow a hospital for the needy citizens of Beaune. Many people gave vineyards to the hospital and the money raised by the sale of their wines supports the poor of the town to this day. The Hôtel-Dieu functioned as a hospital until very recently but the patients are now rehoused and the building is a museum. Allow an hour to see the beautiful, mosaic-tiled, gabled roof, rooms illustrating hospital life, and the extraordinary polyptych by Rogier van der Weyden depicting The Last Judgment. This is a glorious painting and I found myself irritated by the hurried way the guided tour presents it.

The wines made from the Hôtel-Dieu estates, which are known as the Hospices de Beaune, are auctioned during the third weekend of November. This is a major media event, widely covered on French television and seen as a key price indicator for the rest of the vintage. The marathon auction is the excuse for, and centrepiece of, three flamboyant days of banqueting. The 'Trois Glorieuses' or glorious days commence with a dinner at the Château du Clos de Vougeot and end with a lunch party in Meursault the following Monday. This last binge is known as the Paulée, and growers vie with each other to provide the best bottles to accompany the massive multi-course meal.

Avoid this weekend unless you're sure of a bed space. The town swiftly reverts to normal, however, and business and tourism continue quietly as usual. Don't miss the informative Musée du Vin de Bourgogne and the Collégiale Notre-Dame. The church houses a series of beautiful tapestries depicting the life of the Virgin Mary.

I also like to take a walk around the ramparts, which run for about 2km, more or less continuously except for a stretch in the northwest corner. Then it's just a question of wandering the streets, following your nose; it's difficult to get lost and there's plenty of beautiful architecture to attract the eye.

To the north of the town centre are two *négociants* to visit who between them illustrate very neatly the role of the merchant in Burgundy winemaking and wine marketing. If you've been walking or driving around Beaune you can't possibly have missed the signs to the cellars of **PATRIARCHE PÈRE & FILS**: they offer you a visit to 'The biggest cellars in Burgundy'. I do believe these cellars are well worth a tour, although I must be honest and say it's worth it more for the experience of tramping along a kilometre or so of dimly-lit cellars, past stacks of bottles and into a candlelit tasting-room, rather than necessarily for the wines themselves.

Admission costs FF50 and, although they say this fee is donated to charity and the tasting is free, I'm inclined to treat this strictly as a commercial transaction; taste the wines they're showing but don't be seduced by the atmosphere into buying what by daylight may not seem such good value. They give you a *tastevin* to taste in. This is a shallow dish made of silver (or plated) to reflect as much light as possible into the wine when it's being tasted in a dark cellar.

For a very different view of the *négociant*'s role, call at **CHAMPY PÈRE & CIE**. This house was established in 1720, making it the oldest *négociant* in Burgundy, buying in wines for maturation alongside the production of its own vineyards. It was sold in 1989 to the American-owned *négociants* Louis Jadot, but they were only interested in the vineyards; the house and name of Champy were bought by father and son Henri and Pierre Meurgey. They've set about revitalizing the firm and have a very worthwhile selection of wines on sale.

You can taste and buy in an attractive mini-museum, surrounded by collections of winemaking implements. But ask, preferably in advance, to see Vat 17 and the railway, and you'll be taken on a tour of some of the most interesting cellar items in all Burgundy.

Vat 17 is a tasting-room built into an old barrel. There's room for about six inside, complete with table and stools, and walls lined with photographs of celebrities enjoying the facilities. (I gather these days it's used not so much for tasting as for serious drinking.) You can shut the barrel door and no-one would know you were there.

The 'railway', on the other hand, is in the attic, a floor above the vats, and was an integral part of the vinification process a hundred years ago. A decade after phylloxera had devastated Burgundy's vineyards in the 1880s, replanting had produced new vines giving light-coloured juice, which the winemakers didn't know how to handle. The company's head at that time was a friend of Pasteur and he devised the idea of heating the must to 60°C (140°F) (that's the same as for colourfast cottons) to draw out the maximum colour and start the fermentation. Once the cauldron of must was heated, it was rolled along tracks in the roof and poured down into one of the waiting vats in the floor below. There was a lift and other machinery, all powered by steam – you can still see the boiler. The area was last used in 1989 and the last vintage to be boiled up was the '87.

The rest of the buildings and cellars are well worth a visit. The honeycomb of cellars contains bottles dating back to the mid-19th century. With the end of the last century proving to be a strong period for the *négociants*, they had plenty of money to invest in building work. Eiffel (of the Tower) was born in Dijon and his ironwork can be seen here and in the next property to visit, **DOMAINE ALBERT MOROT**.

This is on the outskirts of Beaune, on the D970 in the direction of Saulieu, past the Lycée Viticole (itself open for visitors and to sell the wines made by pupils and teachers). Run by the indomitable Mme Choppin, great-granddaughter of the founder, with just three vine-yard workers, you can taste a selection of well-structured Beaune Premiers Crus. Her generic red Bourgogne is declassified Premier Cru and also good value.

She's helpful with guiding you towards the wines you want to buy, asking whether you are looking for fine wine or a stronger style, wines for drinking now or to keep, and knowledgeable burgundy fans will be able to learn a great deal from her. Her barrel cellars, supported by Eiffel ironwork, are above vaulted bottle storage cellars. Wine, from the ground-level open fermentation vats (*pigeage* done by feet), is fed down to the barrels by gravity – there's no pumping to upset the wine, and no filtration either.

Mme Choppin will sell you wine practically any time: 'If my door is closed people open it, so it's easier to leave it open'. Saves having to beat it down.

For a panoramic view of Beaune and its vineyards continue along the D970 and turn right up to the Montagne de Beaune. Then retrace your steps to the ring-road and turn south onto the N74. The road divides as you clear the suburbs and you should turn right onto the D973 to Pommard, but before doing this fans of cooperatives may like to turn left into the CAVES DES HAUTES-CÔTES.

The modern sales area has plenty of wines available to taste, although when I visited some were a little faded after being open too long. This is the major outlet for wines from the Hautes Côtes and is a source of good-quality, basic-level generics. You can also buy wine *en vrac*, with corks and labels thrown in.

Now follow the D973 to **Pommard**. My heart never fails to lift as I follow this road out into the vines, with its trail of famous names. On the outskirts is the CHÂTEAU DE POMMARD, an imposing 18th century building and one of the few châteaux in Burgundy, in an enclosed vineyard. A tasting and tour costs FF20. The wine is a good *village* wine, but not cheap at FF157 the bottle upwards. Luckily, as this is a paid tasting, you need feel under no obligation to buy.

Head next into the village, park in the central square and look for the signposts to DOMAINE ANDRÉ MUSSY. M Mussy is 79, and I confidently expect him to be around to welcome you for the lifetime of this book; he's a walking advertisement for the life-enhancing properties of working with vines and wine. He speaks no English but if your French is up to it you can learn much about his philosophy and discuss it with him. Descend into his cellars on an industrial platform-lift. Space is limited, filled to the brim with barrels and bottles. He keeps yields low, and practises minimum intervention in the cellar – fining with egg-whites, filtering only if necessary, without pumping to tire the wine. He is very conscious of the weight of history; he's the 11th generation of a family going back to 1746, and 1993 was his 67th vinification. His son-in-law is gradually taking over from him. These wines are very attractive and fairly priced, and this is an excellent visit for advanced students. Pommard's wines are fuller and heavier than either of its neighbours' and Mussy makes excellent examples.

On the square you'll also find a shop, Les Domaines de Pommard, which sells the wines of 16 producers at cellar prices. Some of these are very good indeed, such as those from Jean Garaudet and Virely Arcelain. No English is spoken here.

The next stop is **Volnay**, home of lighter, silky reds. It's worth parking in the square for a stroll around this ancient village, the only one on the Côte to be sited above its vineyards.

From Volnay drop down into **Meursault** and be prepared to get lost in its meandering maze of roads. **CHÂTEAU DE MEURSAULT** is owned by the same group as Patriarche (qv), and the two visits have several things in common: a paid tour, a route through atmospheric cellars, a souvenir *tastevin* and a selection of wines to taste. There is also a small modern art gallery. Again, take advantage of the fact that this is a paid tasting; you may find a wine here that's very much to your taste but, if you don't, you are under no obligation to buy. It's dear, too; Aligoté for FF59 is the cheapest white and prices rise to a stratospheric FF450 for Meursault.

Tasting on a more human scale is available every afternoon from grower and *négociant* **JEAN GERMAIN**. His capable English-speaking staff offer very good wines and advice from a small tasting-room.

The large *négociant* house of Antonin Rodet (qv), based in Mercurey on the Côte Chalonnaise, has a 50% interest in the Meursault domaine of **JACQUES PRIEUR**. Quality has greatly improved since this *négociant* became involved, and you can arrange a visit via Rodet's offices (see Listings page 115). There's plenty to see, not least the pneumatic *pigeage* equipment.

From Meursault head for **Puligny-Montrachet**. Meursault and Puligny, together with Chassagne-Montrachet two minutes away, are responsible for the great white wines of Burgundy. I don't find the village itself of great interest and think it's much more fun to get out among the vines, on foot or by bike, and see the Grand Cru Montrachet vineyards. These are situated above the village and offer another photo-opportunity with a walled gate.

This is the home of the most expensive dry white wine in the world, retailing in the UK for perhaps £700 a bottle. Who pays this kind of money? American wine-writer Robert Parker points to persistent rumours that there's a big market for it among the drug barons of Miami, although he notes that given their short life expectancy they're unlikely to wait for it to age properly. (In south London, the equivalent tipple seems to be Moët & Chandon. A poor second, if you ask me.)

Parker also relates a story about a Second World War French general fighting the Germans as they retreated through the Burgundy vineyards. Apparently he wouldn't attack them while they were in the Grand Cru vineyards for fear of damaging the precious vines. Only when he heard the Germans had moved down to the inferior lower slopes would he give the order to open fire. A similar attitude was demonstrated more recently when the French government amended the route of the A6 motorway to avoid the Montrachet vineyards.

From Puligny, turn right onto the N6 and turn off again almost immediately into Gamay, the village that named the grape. Next along is **St-Aubin**, an underestimated *appellation* full of dynamic young growers making very fine wine. Typical of these is **HENRI PRUDHON**, who offers remarkably good wines at very fair prices indeed, such as a St-Aubin Premier Cru for FF54. No English is spoken, although the son is learning. St-Aubin's steep, narrow, winding streets are worth exploring on foot.

Climb out of St-Aubin on the D33 (it's signposted Route des Hautes Côtes) and you can look back on some lovely, wide valley views. You also pass the château of La Rochepot, with its Burgundy-tiled roof. Turn right in La Rochepot, and left shortly after onto the D17I. The route is signposted Cluny à Beaune par la Vignoble. There are waymarked walks in Baubigny and the road passes through Orches, clinging to the side of the mountain. Look out for the parking area above **St-Romain**, where the views are quite stunning.

Now you can either drop down into St-Romain, where attractions include a marked trail up to the 13th century castle, or continue along the extremely pretty D17 into Pommard. Head back into Beaune, if that's where you're staying.

Otherwise head for Meursault, via Monthélie and Auxey-Duresses, and down to the N74. I'm not usually keen on taking the main roads but this one is exceptional; as you drive towards Chagny you'll see a quite beautiful panorama of the Côte unfolding. It's lovely even in winter, as curls of smoke rise from the little portable braziers, looking like punctured wheelbarrows, used to burn vine prunings. Incidentally there's a bustling restaurant on the other side of the N74 in Meursault. Follow the signs to the railway station and you'll find the Relais de la Diligence à la Gare, where the food is good, plentiful (of course) and remarkably cheap.

Follow the N74 under the N6 and turn off to **Santenay**. This sprawling, attractive village is the last major stop on the Côte d'Or (strictly speaking, the last port of call is Cheilly-lès-Maranges). The village is in two parts, lower and upper. Nestled in among the upper village houses is **DOMAINE PRIEUR-BRUNET**, with its distinctive, tiled roof. I can't recommend this visit highly enough. For a start, the wines are splendid and remarkably well priced: generic red for FF31, Santenay Maladière Premier Cru for FF63 to FF82, depending on the vintage. The whites, too, are excellent, including Santenay Clos Rousseau Premier Cru for FF74–94 and Meursault-Charmes Premier Cru for FF102–121.

Parts of the cellars are 15th century but much of the building is new. They are adherents of the cool maceration school and even chill the whites to -3°C (27°F) for a week to precipitate the tartrates – which is somewhat interventionist but the wines don't seem to have suffered. Visits include a cellar tour as a matter of course and there's a comfortable, well-lit tasting-room. These wines are concentrated, rich and well balanced, at prices very favourable for the quality. Dominique Prieur speaks excellent English and pitches the visit at your level of knowledge. Sassy, attractive wines.

From Santenay cross the canal and turn right onto the D974. This quiet road follows the Canal du Centre, popular for narrow-boat holidays. Cruisers like the next stop, the **CAVES DE CHEILLY**, on the D974 just outside **Cheilly-lès-Maranges**, because they can fill up with wine from the top burgundy *appellations* to vino very *ordinaire* at FF8 the litre.

Although it sounds like a cooperative, the Caves de Cheilly mainly sells the produce of one man, René Martin. It does offer higher *appellations* from other producers, but more to fill out the range for the holiday-makers than as a serious sales drive. M Martin's admirable assistant, Nathalie de Grange, speaks good English and will show you the cellars (selling, not working, space with large vats of *en vrac* wines) and explain as much as you'd like to know about the area, its wines and its tourist attractions. Maranges is a new *appellation*, seldom seen; there are good examples at the Caves plus honestly-made generics. It's a friendly, easy place to visit – right on the main road, with easy parking and help if you need it.

Cheilly is officially still part of the Golden Slope but it doesn't feel like it. The scenery has changed, we're moving into the more mixed agricultural setting of the Côte Chalonnaise.

EXPLORING THE CÔTE CHALONNAISE

The nearest place to stay is the Auberge du Camp Romain in **Chassey-le-Camp**; this is a rapidly developing tourist hotel offering modern, quiet, very good value rooms with a view right out across the valley. There's an outdoor pool (barbecues in summer) and there'll soon be an indoor one, too. I wish they'd get a new chef, though; the food lets them down and the wine list is a disgrace. (It's a perfect illustration of the pitfalls of choosing Burgundy wine.) But stick to basic dishes and house wine, and you'll have a peaceful, reasonably-priced stay.

At the other end of the scale there's the imposing Hostellerie du Château de Bellecroix, off the N6 south of **Chagny**, with elegant, expensive bedrooms and the prettiest dining-room I encountered in Burgundy, set in the great hall. I ate a very enjoyable meal, aided by a splendid waiter with a real sense of theatre.

In **Rully** there's the Hôtel Commerce, with Restaurant Le Vendangerot (the grape-picker's basket). This is a small establishment, with rooms traditionally furnished, slightly faded but great on atmosphere and value. The food is of a high standard and the wines (including by the carafe, rare in Burgundy) are very reasonable.

Mercurey has the Hôtellerie du Val d'Or. There's a very friendly welcome here. The food gets a Michelin star and has a strong regional accent, with the emphasis on game in season and offal. Their desserts are brilliant; I must mention the *soufflé glacé*, which had a creaminess the likes of which I haven't tasted since I was about six. Caveat: sound insulation in the rooms is poor and the hall floors are very creaky.

Finally, in **Givry**, there's Hôtel de la Halle, long popular with the British for honest regional cooking and over-decorated bedrooms at tiny prices.

I mention all these places at the start of the section to give you an overview. There's a good variation of price and you can pick one as your base for visiting all the properties or move around as you wish. (You could even, if you've become addicted to Beaune, an understandable affliction, travel out to the Côte Chalonnaise from there; the drive from Beaune to Chagny takes about 15 minutes.)

The first wine village to visit is **Bouzeron**. This village is best known for producing the most successful wine from Burgundy's lesser white grape, the Aligoté. This success is recognized: the village, alone of Aligoté winemakers, may put its name on the label as AC Bourgogne Aligoté de Bouzeron. The village is also a good source of well-priced generic red and white.

The finest maker of Aligoté de Bouzeron is **A & P DE VILLAINE**, part owner of the Domaine de la Romanée Conti which makes <u>the</u> most expensive wines of Burgundy. The Aligoté is priced at the other end of the scale, but is still excellent. The generic reds and whites are also well worth having. This is not a visit I've yet been able to make, but the wines are widely available in the UK and I've often enjoyed them.

The **DOMAINE DE LA FOLIE**, just off the D981 on the outskirts of Bouzeron (officially it's in Chagny) will sell you a lively, fresh Aligoté and also some well-made Rully whites. They also make an extraordinary cassis liqueur. The domaine charges a small sum if you only want to taste, but if you buy a dozen bottles you get one free, and other quantity discounts can be negotiated.

From Bouzeron head for the village of **Rully**, dominated by an impressive château. Antonin Rodet (qv) makes **CHÂTEAU DE RULLY** wine and you can arrange a visit through his firm (see Listings page 115).

In the village itself **MICHEL BRIDAY** is establishing himself as a wine-maker with a growing reputation. His vineyards are all rented – he can't afford to buy and anyway no-one's selling. He invests every spare penny in improving his equipment and cellars, which he's built up from scratch over the last 15 years. His difficulties illustrate the problems of the would-be winemaker without a family holding to inherit. It's generally accepted that Rully's whites are better than its reds and that the reverse is the case for Mercurey, but here I found the Rully reds more successful than the whites.

From Rully there are two pretty routes to **Mercurey** but neither is well-signposted, so it may end up being pot luck which you take. One runs down behind the Château de Rully to Aluze, from where you turn left onto the D978. The other meanders southeast, bringing you out on a hill east of the village (keep turning right).

Mercurey at first sight seems to be little other than a long, dull main drag; but get off the main road and climb up into the village and you'll find a charming spot. There are some very attractive walks in the vineyards either side of the village; nothing is waymarked, just follow your instinct.

The two properties to visit in Mercurey are next door to each other but they couldn't be more different. **DOMAINE JEAN MARÉCHAL** makes only red wines: a generic Bourgogne Rouge, Mercurey and a *cuvée prestige*, with prices ranging from FF36 to FF60. M Maréchal works with extreme care and pride in his job, and gives freely of his time to visitors who come to taste: 'If you love your work you have pleasure in sharing it with others'.

I watched him packing wine into boxes with great precision, not reaching for the sealing tape until the edges of the box were perfectly aligned. Such care over a small detail reflects his meticulous wine-making. He prefers a long, slow fermentation, believing that quick fermentation gives short-term aromas in bottle but nothing for the long term. If you speak good French, have plenty of time and want to know the fine detail of a winemaker's philosophy, don't hesitate to visit here.

Just next door is the house of *négociant* and grower **ANTONIN RODET**. Rodet can take a large part of the credit for gaining greater recognition for Côte Chalonnaise wines. Call here for a tasting and you might feel you've entered someone's elegant home (it was indeed the first house built by the founder). You'll be escorted downstairs to a small, attractive tasting-cellar, where you can try wines from Rodet's properties, Château de Chamirey in Mercurey, Château de Rully (qv) and Domaine Jacques Prieur in Meursault (qv). You can make appointments to visit all these properties by phoning Rodet, and they are all well worth the visit. At Château de Chamirey, for instance, you can see yet another *pigeage* system: internal paddles agitate the grape-skin cap several times a day.

This is winemaking of excellent quality, a fact that hasn't gone unnoticed among major restaurants and airlines, where Rodet has found an important market. You won't meet the winemaker at Rodet's tasting-cellars (although you may well if you visit the domaines – there's an oenologist at each), but you'll get an insight into an organization which is becoming a significant player in the region and is still selling very good value wines.

One word of warning: beware of going to Michel Juillot's estate, on the other side of the road. They were so worried about upsetting their importers by selling direct to us Brits that it was all I could do to extract a price list.

Leaving Mercurey towards Chalon-sur-Saône, turn off right past the Château de Chamirey and head towards Givry via **St-Martin**, **St-Jean** and **Jambles**. This partly follows the official wine route and you may see some signposts. It's a very attractive road, through rolling country-side with mixed agriculture and vines only on certain favoured slopes.

From Jambles you can cut across to Givry, or head down to **Buxy** and its **CAVES DES VIGNERONS**. This is a large, modern cooperative that will sell you wines from the pump, or well-made Montagny – elegant, reasonably-priced white wines. Montagny is the southern-most *appellation* on the Côte Chalonnaise and, alone of all French wines, can call itself Grand Cru solely on alcohol content; if it reaches 11.5% it's a Grand Cru. Rodet (qv) also offers excellent examples of Montagny.

If you'd like to step back in time, go to St-Gengoux-le-National, south of Buxy, off the D981. There's a branch of the Buxy co-op there, as dank and old-fashioned as the head office is bright and modern. I loved it.

Head north now, or across, to **Givry** for the wines of **DOMAINE THÉNARD**. Here you can buy red or white Givry, both extremely well made and excellent value. You can also visit the estate's 14th century cellars by arrangement (it's easier off-season, when the work-force isn't out in the vineyards). I've bought very reliable wine here for several years.

Givry is plagued by a one-way system; if you've passed the Hôtel de la Halle, then you've missed the turning for Thénard, so keep turning left until it comes up again. After Givry the tour is complete. The D981 will take you straight up to all points north.

Listings

When telephoning France from the UK, the number must be preceded by the digits 010 33. Producers are listed in wine route order, and hotels/restaurants by town or village according to the route. Accommodation prices are per room, meal prices are per head.

Producers

Domaine Denis Mortet
22 rue de l'Eglise,
21220 Gevrey-Chambertin
Tel 80 34 10 05, Fax 80 58 51 32
Visits by appointment Mon–Sat 9–12,
14–18; closed Sun
Credit cards accepted
Some English

Domaine Dujac
7 rue de la Bussière,
21220 Morey-St-Denis
Tel 80 34 32 58, Fax 80 51 89 76
Visits by appointment
Good English

Château du Clos de Vougeot
21640 Vougeot
Tel 80 62 86 09, Fax 80 62 82 75
Open April–Sept Mon–Sun 9–18.30
incl lunch-time; Oct–March 9–11.30,
14–17.30; closes Sat at 17.00
(admission FF15)
Tours available in English (can book)

Château de la Tour
21640 Vougeot
Tel 80 62 86 13, Fax 80 62 82 72
Open Easter–Nov Mon–Sun 9–12,
14–18; visits by appointment in winter
Credit cards accepted
Good English

Domaine Armelle & Bernard Rion
8 Route Nationale,
21700 Vosne-Romanée
Tel 80 61 05 31, Fax 80 61 34 60
Open Mon–Sat 9–12, 14–18;
occasionally open Sun
Credit cards accepted
Some English

Domaine Bertrand Ambroise
Rue de l'Eglise,
21700 Premeaux-Prissey
Tel 80 62 30 19, Fax 80 62 38 69
Open Mon–Sat pm;
appointment preferred
Credit cards accepted
Good English

Domaine Tollot-Beaut & Fils
Rue Alexandre Tollot,
21200 Chorey-lès-Beaune
Tel 80 22 16 54, Fax 80 22 12 61
Visits by appointment Mon–Sat;
closed Sun
Good English

Domaine Jacques Germain
Le Château, 21200 Chorey-lès-Beaune
Tel 80 22 06 05, Fax 80 24 03 93
Open Mon–Sun 9–12, 14–19;
appointment preferred for extended visit
Credit cards accepted
Good English

Patriarche Père & Fils
7 rue du College, 21200 Beaune
Open Mon–Sun 9.30–11.30, 14–17.30;
closed 15 Dec–1 March
(admission Mon–Sat FF50, Sun FF80)
Some English

Champy Père & Cie
5 rue du Grenier à Sel, 21200 Beaune
Tel 80 24 97 30, Fax 80 24 97 40
Open Mon–Fri 9–12, 14–18
Credit cards accepted
Good English

Domaine Albert Morot
Château de la Creusotte, 21200 Beaune
Tel 80 22 35 39, Fax 80 22 47 50
Open Mon–Sun 10–12, 14–18;
appointment preferred
Credit cards accepted
Good English

Les Caves des Hautes-Côtes
Route de Pommard, 21200 Beaune
Tel 80 24 63 12, Fax 80 22 87 06
Open Mon–Sat 9–12, 14–18;
5 April–21 Nov also open Sun 9–12
No English

Château de Pommard
21630 Pommard
Tel 80 22 07 99
Open 1 April–22 Nov Mon–Sun 9–18
incl lunch-time; closed winter
(admission FF20)
Some English

Domaine André Mussy
Rue Dauphin, 21630 Pommard
Tel 80 22 05 56, Fax 80 24 07 47
Open Mon–Sat 9.30–12, 14.30–19;
visits by appointment Sun
No English

Château de Meursault
21190 Meursault
Tel 80 21 22 98, Fax 80 21 66 77
Open Mon–Sun 9.30–12, 14.30–18
(admission FF50)
Some English

Maison Jean Germain
11 rue de Lattre-de-Tassigny,
21190 Meursault
Tel 80 21 63 67, Fax 80 21 64 66
Open Mon–Fri pm;
visits by appointment in winter
Credit cards accepted
Some English

Domaine Henri Prudhon & Fils
Place de l'Eglise, 21190 St-Aubin
Tel 80 21 31 33/80 21 36 70
Visits by appointment Mon–Sun
No English

Domaine Prieur-Brunet
Rue de Narosse, 21590 Santenay
Tel 80 20 60 56, Fax 80 20 64 31
Open Easter–Nov Mon–Sun; appoint-
ment preferred, essential in winter
Credit cards accepted
Good English

Caves de Cheilly
Cheilly-lès-Maranges, 71150 Chagny
Tel 85 91 14 51, Fax 85 91 17 57
Open Mon–Sat 9.30–12, 14.30–18.30,
Sun 10–12, 15–19
Credit cards accepted
Some English

A & P de Villaine
71150 Bouzeron
Tel 85 91 20 50, Fax 85 87 04 10
Visits (strictly) by appointment Mon–Fri
8–12, 14–17
Good English (from Mme de Villaine)

Domaine de la Folie
Route de Rully, 71150 Chagny
Tel 85 87 18 59, Fax 85 87 03 53
Open Mon–Sat 9–12, 14–17, Sun 11–13
(tasting FF30, refundable with purchase)
Some English

Domaine Michel Briday
Grande Rue, 71150, Rully
Tel 85 87 07 90, Fax 85 91 25 68
Open Mon–Sun 9–12, 14–18
Credit cards accepted
Some English

Domaine Jean Maréchal
Route Nationale, 71640 Mercurey
Tel 85 45 11 29, Fax 85 45 18 52
Open Mon–Sat 8–12.30, 13.30–19.30;
visits by appointment Sun
No English

Antonin Rodet
Route Nationale, 71640 Mercury
Tel 85 45 22 22, Fax 85 45 25 49
Open May–Oct Mon–Fri 9–12, 14–18;
visits by appointment in winter
Credit cards accepted
Good English
Visits by appointment with Rodet:
Domaine Jacques Prieur, Château de
Rully, Château de Chamirey

Caves des Vignerons de Buxy
Les Vignes de la Croix, 71390 Buxy
(& 71460 St-Gengoux-le-National)
Tel 85 92 03 03
Open Mon–Sat 8.15–12, 14–18;
closed Tues at St-Gengoux
No English

Domaine Thénard
7 rue de l'Hôtel de Ville, 71640 Givry
Tel 85 44 31 36
Open Mon–Sat 8–19 incl lunch;

visits by appointment in winter to *cave*
No English

Hotels and Restaurants
H Hotel   **R** Restaurant

Gevrey-Chambertin
H Les Grands Crus
Route des Grands Crus,
21220 Gevrey-Chambertin
Tel 80 34 34 15, Fax 80 51 89 07
FF330–410

R Bonbistrot
Rue Chambertin
Tel 80 34 33 20
FF100–150

R Les Millésimes
25 rue Eglise
Tel 80 51 84 24
FF295–560

R Le Petit Caveau
4 rue Richebourg
Tel 80 34 32 83
FF80–140

R La Sommellerie
7 rue Souvert
Tel 80 34 31 48
FF130–360

Fixin
R Au Relais de l'Empereur
35 route des Grands Crus
Tel 80 52 45 46
FF68–140

Flagey-Echézeaux
R Robert Losset
Place Eglise
Tel 80 62 88 10
FF95–250 incl wine

Nuits-St-Georges
HR Hôtel La Gentilhommière
13 Vallée Serrée, Route Meuilley,
21700 Nuits-St-Georges
Tel 80 61 12 06, Fax 80 61 30 33
Rooms FF400, Meals FF180–240

Savigny-lès-Beaune
HR L'Ouvrée
Route de Bouilland,
21420 Savigny-lès-Beaune
Tel 80 21 51 52, Fax 80 26 10 04
Rooms FF220–250, Meals FF92–220

Bouilland
HR Le Vieux Moulin
21420 Bouilland
Tel 80 21 51 16, Fax 80 21 59 90
Rooms FF380–800, Meals FF190–500

Beaune
HR Central
2 rue V-Millot, 21200 Beaune
Tel 80 24 77 24, Fax 80 22 30 40
Rooms FF330–450, Meals FF99–185

HR Hôtel de la Poste
1 boulevard Clémenceau, 21200 Beaune
Tel 80 22 08 11, Fax 80 24 19 71
Rooms FF500–850, Meals FF160–320

H Hostellerie de la Bretonnière
43 rue de fg Bretonnière, 21200 Beaune
Tel 80 22 15 77, Fax 80 22 72 54
FF175–350

R Le Bistrot Bourguignon
Rue Monge
Dishes up to FF40, Meals FF60

R La Ciboulette
69 rue Lorraine
Tel 80 24 70 72
FF82–112

R Le Jardin des Remparts
10 rue Hôtel-Dieu
Tel 80 24 79 41
FF125–290

Meursault
R Relais de la Diligence à la Gare
(opposite the station)
Tel 80 21 21 32
FF63–148

Chassey-le-Camp
HR Auberge du Camp Romain
71150 Chassey-le-Camp
Tel 85 87 09 91, Fax 85 87 11 51
Rooms FF138–320, Meals FF113–164

Chagny
HR Hostellerie du Château
de Bellecroix
71150 Chagny
Tel 85 87 13 86, Fax 85 91 28 62
Rooms FF550–920, Meals FF220–330
(member of Relais du Silence)

Rully
HR Hôtel Commerce &
Restaurant Le Vendangerot
Place Ste-Marie,
71150 Rully
Tel 85 87 20 09
Rooms FF140–250, Meals FF70–160

Mercurey
HR Hôtellerie du Val d'Or
Grande Rue, 71640 Mercurey
Tel 85 45 13 70, Fax 85 45 18 45
Rooms FF310–390, Meals FF160–370

Givry
HR Hôtel de la Halle
Place de la Halle, 71640 Givry
Tel 85 44 32 45
Rooms FF200–230, Meals FF55–205

Champagne

Champagne is a pretty miserable place. It rains nearly half the year – for 160 days on average. It's cold, damp and often misty. The average temperature is a meagre 10°C (50°F). It produces thin, neutral, acidic, low-alcohol wines. If someone hadn't worked out how to put bubbles in the bottle the wine wouldn't have a great deal going for it, but someone did. Now Champagne makes some of the world's most expensive wines, and has attached to these an aura of glamour, celebration, sophistication and extravagance. Pretty clever stuff, eh?

Attila the Hun fought a major battle on the plains of Champagne in the 5th century AD, and the First World War's first Battle of the Marne laid waste to the vineyards just before the 1914 harvest. In between these acts of war there are two important names to know in the romantic version of Champagne's winemaking history: Dom Pérignon, a 17th century monk, and Veuve Clicquot, who lived a century later.

To start with, the wines sparkled by accident and bubbles were frowned upon as a fault. The wine would stop fermenting in vat in the cold of winter and start again after it had been bottled, when the cellars warmed up in spring, trapping the carbon dioxide given off by the fermenting yeast. The wines themselves, from red grapes, were probably an insipid pink in colour, weak and harsh.

Dom Pérignon changed all that. Although he may not have been the person who sorted out the making-it-sparkling question, which is a shame for fans of romantic legend, he was certainly responsible for developing the art of blending wines from different areas and vintages to make a smoother end product, and for maturing the wine long enough for it to acquire a mature richness. He also made white wine from red grapes by using very gentle pressing.

Dom Pérignon showed how to turn a problem – weak, insipid sparkling wines – into an advantage. (Admittedly he was helped by the English invention of stronger, more reliable bottles.) Later champagne makers learned how to control production of the bubbles, and how to remove the by-products of the process, which is where Mme Clicquot comes in.

All wine ferments once – that's what creates the alcohol. Champagne ferments a second time while in bottle, but these days it's no longer an accident. Technologists have worked out how to induce a second fermentation by adding a dose of sugar and yeast to a bottle of once-fermented wine. The dose is carefully regulated: too little and you have a very weak sparkle, too much and the bottle explodes under the pressure.

The yeast creates bubbles; it also leaves dead cells, or lees, at the bottom of the bottle. For years champagne was drunk 'off its lees' because no-one could work out how to remove them. You had to be very careful how you poured the wine, or the lees would cloud it (it was worse than pouring White Shield). Then Widow Clicquot and her cellar-master invented the *pupitre*, a hinged board with holes cut into it at a 45° angle. Legend has it that she devised the prototype by cutting holes in her kitchen table.

You put the bottles in the holes horizontally and every day give them a jolting twist, which gradually, over two or three months, raises them until they stand vertically on their corks. The jolt loosens the sticky lees from the side of the bottle, the twist turns the bottle upright, easing the lees onto the cork. The process is known as *remuage*, inadequately translated as 'riddling'. Then you disgorge the lees. The original method simply allowed the cork to shoot out of the bottle and wasted some of the wine as well as removing the dead yeast cells. Today, you freeze the sediment into a pellet by upending the bottle neck into a brine bath. Open the bottle and the pellet flies out, complete with all the unwanted lees. Then you top up the bottle with a *dosage* of wine and sugar and recork it. Simple, really.

While all these refinements to the technical process were taking place, the champagne sales force wasn't idle. Zany stunts and flamboyant salesmen created the image that no party was complete without champagne. At the same time, the great champagne houses were formed. With the wine's increasing success, vineyards were planted beyond the original area, including in the Aube to the south-east. The big houses even began to buy in grapes from outside the region. A series of riots followed as irate growers tried to establish who was allowed to make champagne – at which point the First World War intervened. The Second World War saw the occupation of Reims and the formation of the CIVC, an inter-professional committee created to liaise with the occupying German army. It now represents the interests of champagne at home and abroad.

WHO MAKES THE WINE?

After the war, sales grew rapidly and the advertising efforts of the big houses established their names worldwide. Today many of the most illustrious names are owned by multinational conglomerates and 'traded like playing Monopoly', as one grower put it.

At the other end of the spectrum you find the small-scale champagne maker, who bottles the wine made from his or her own vineyard. In between come the cooperatives and a huge group of nearly 20,000 growers who own on average little more than a hectare each and who sell grapes to the big houses and the cooperatives. Relatively few growers own enough land under vine to make a living from it.

You can tell from the label who has made your wine if you know how to decode the abbreviations used, as listed below. These are handy to remember because over 10,000 champagne brands, or different names, appear on the labels. (The figures in brackets show approximately how many brand names there are in each category.)

RM (Récoltant-Manipulant) A grower producing champagne from his or her own grapes (3,000)

RC (Récoltant-Coopérateur) A grower selling wine made by a cooperative (3,350)

R (Récoltant) A small-scale grower producing up to a maximum of 500 bottles a year under his or her own name (12)

ND (Négociant-Distributeur) A *récoltant* wishing to become a little more commercial can use these initials (8)

SR (Société de Récoltant) The term used by a company created by growers from the same family. The number of these is expected to increase (17)

The above list gives a total of about 6,500 individual grower labels.

NM (Négociant-Manipulant) A champagne house (1,170)

CM (Coopérative de Manipulation) A cooperative (200)

MA (Marque d'Acheteur) The term for shops' or restaurants' own-label brands, ie the buyer's own brand (2,500)

Since there are over 10,000 brands in total, you can't learn all the names, but the abbreviations at least tell you whether the wine was made by a grower, a *négociant* or a co-op, or, in the UK high street, if it has a name invented by a supermarket. RC, for instance, is a particularly cheeky one: the label will give every appearance of the wine being a grower's champagne, when in fact it was made by a co-op.

Twenty-eight of the champagne houses have formed themselves into a marketing group known as the Grandes Marques, or 'great brands'. This doesn't mean they're the best on offer, it's simply a name. Some great houses are members, but other equally fine houses are not – and a few members could be said to be trading on past glory rather than present quality.

A number of the champagne houses own vineyards, others buy in grapes; some, like Moët & Chandon, do both. Each will tell you its way is best. Vineyard owners say they can control quality from start to finish and are not dependent on the vagaries of the market; buyers-in point to the flexibility of being able to choose only the best grapes on offer and of being able to buy according to the quality of the harvest, of not being landed with loads of underripe or rotten grapes, say, in a bad year. Take your pick.

HOW THE WINES ARE CLASSIFIED

Champagne is made from three grape varieties: Chardonnay, Pinot Noir and Pinot Meunier. The two Pinots are black grapes and together account for roughly three-quarters of planting. If you see *blanc de blancs* (white of whites) on the label, the wine has been made only from the white grape, Chardonnay. *Blanc de noirs*, conversely, is made only from black grapes. You can make white wine from black grapes (with care) but you can't, of course, make red wine from white grapes. Pressing the black grapes gently and quickly ensures that next to no colouring escapes from the skins.

Rosé champagne is made either by allowing more colour to come out of the black grape-skins, or by making a separate still red wine and blending it in before bottling. Some still red wines are sold, called Coteaux Champenois; the village of Bouzy is best known for them. I think they are wildly overpriced in most cases. There's also a still pink wine, Rosé des Riceys, made at Les Riceys in the Aube.

The region's main product, by a huge margin, is white champagne. Most of this is NV, non-vintage. Strictly speaking this isn't an accurate definition, as the blend is probably made up of wines from several vintages, but the term serves to distinguish non-vintage from vintage champagne, which does put a year on the label and must be made exclusively of wines from that vintage. The vintage champagnes are more expensive and need to spend much longer in bottle as they don't have the softening influence of older wines to help them along.

Top of the quality ladder is the *cuvée de prestige*, or deluxe champagne. Led by Moët's prestige brand, Dom Pérignon, most houses make an expensive, top-of-the-range wine. Unless you don't need to ask the price, I would suggest steering clear of these as better value is usually to be had elsewhere.

There are three wine districts in what the big houses would like you to think of as the 'classic' area of champagne, the Marne, and of these only two are held in really high esteem. The Montagne de Reims is between Reims and Epernay, the Côte des Blancs lies to the south of Epernay, and the Vallée de la Marne is to the west of Epernay.

The last of these is looked down on because it grows mostly the less-favoured Pinot Meunier grape. When you tour the big champagne houses, you'll be surprised how often you hear that the house uses no Pinot Meunier, or that it has no holdings in the Vallée de la Marne and other unfashionable areas. Meunier accounts for over a third of all planting, however, so somebody must be using it. Why don't they admit it?

So unfashionable as to be beyond the pale are the other two regions, Sézannais and the Aube. The Aube is so unregarded that it doesn't even merit inclusion on the wine route. I think differently; there are some very good wines being made down there, and because the area is unfashionable the wines are much better value. The Aube lies closer to Chablis than to Epernay, so I've included it as part of The Golden Triangle wine route.

Back in the fashionable end, the growers and houses have established a pecking-order for which villages produce the best grapes. This is called the Echelle des Crus, the 'ladder of villages', and is divided up on a percentile basis. Top of the heap, the best villages are said to be Grands Crus and rank at 100%. Each year, up to 1990, the CIVC fixed a price per kilogram for the grapes, and this was the price the 100% villages got. Moving down the scale, villages rated between 99 and 90%, the Premiers Crus, received the equivalent percentage of the price, and so on down the ladder. The price was fixed according to the expected size and quality of the harvest but also took into account the level of unsold stock lying in Reims cellars and the current world economic situation – 'charging what the market will bear', again.

This system was abolished with the intention of letting market forces rule. Now a 'reference price' is announced, but people follow it almost as closely as the old regulated price and continue to use the percentage scale. Grapes can account for up to £6 of the bottle's price. That's just one reason champagne is so expensive.

The Champagne way of making wines sparkle – second fermentation in bottle – has been adopted as the top method all over the world and until recently has been acknowledged as such on labels with the term *méthode champenoise*, champagne method.

Is imitation the sincerest form of flattery? Not a bit of it. So jealous of their own region's product are the Champenois that they have succeeded in forbidding the rest of the world from using the name of champagne to describe the production process. Now others making sparkling wine by this method must describe their wine in a different way. The term currently adopted by most is 'traditional method'.

WHAT YOU'LL SEE IN THE CELLAR

The champagne method of making sparkling wine, or the traditional method for that matter, offers the most to see in the cellar. It's a closely controlled process.

Regulations determine the yield, in other words the weight of grapes you can grow per hectare, and the amount of juice you can press from a given weight. These rules have recently been tightened up so that 160kg of fruit, rather than 150kg, may produce a maximum of 1hl of juice. That means the grapes are pressed less hard to release the juice. There was also a difference before between the first-pressed juice, which is the best quality and known as the *cuvée*, and the second and third pressings, known as the *premier* and *deux-ième tailles*. Now there is only one *taille*. (The second *taille*, in particular, used to produce pretty inferior wine.) Grand champagne houses will tell you during their tours that they, of course, only use the *cuvée* for their wines; but somebody somewhere must be using the *taille*.

The law also states that grapes must be picked by hand in Champagne so that the grape-skins are unbroken when they arrive at the press house. Some press houses, such as Ayala's (qv) in Ay, are exactly designed to deal with the old pressing equation. The traditional vertical champagne press holds 4,000kg of grapes, and if you go down beneath one you'll see concrete containers for collecting the precise amount of juice that was permissible at each stage. Ayala positively welcomes harvest visitors, and I watched teams of workers moving between the old wooden presses, dismantling and cleaning them between operations. Modern presses can be set automatically to produce the correct quantities of juice for each stage.

The juice, or must, rests in a holding tank for a day or so to let any particles settle, then it's fermented. Almost everybody uses stainless steel these days, with more, or less, sophisticated temperature-regulation equipment. The finest wines, however, are generally believed to be those fermented in oak barrels. (The Champagne *pièce* holds 205 litres, which equates to the 2,050 litres of *cuvée* juice which used to form the first pressing – ten barrels' worth. All very handy.) Top champagne house Krug ferments in barrel, and so do two of the producers recommended below, Vilmart and Alfred Gratien. Fashions change, and producers are gradually returning to the idea of barrel fermentation, at least for their top wines. It's worth looking out in the cellar to see what your host's philosophy is.

Frequently the wine is chaptalized. In other words, extra sugar is added to boost the grape's often poor natural sugar content. Chaptalization is rather like reading the *News of the World*: I won't admit to it, but of course there are a lot of other people who do it all the time. It's not the kind of thing that's brought up easily in the course of polite cellar conversation.

Once first fermentation is over the wine might 'do the malo'. (Not every producer believes in softening the wine by malolactic fermentation, allowing sharp malic acid to soften into smoother lactic acid.) Malo or no, at this point you have a fermented wine. It's low in alcohol because Champagne is so far north that the grapes don't get the chance to ripen as fully as elsewhere. It's also thin and neutral, which paradoxically is just what you need for champagne. Too alcoholic a base wine and you'd have too boozy a brew once you'd fermented it again – the bottle fermentation sends the alcohol content up as well as making bubbles; it also reduces acidity, so you need a bitingly acidic wine to start with.

One of champagne's most distinctive characteristics is the biscuity, yeasty taste and smell that come from the second fermentation. Too strong a base wine and these delicate aromas and flavours would be overwhelmed. So champagne makes a virtue out of necessity twice over, and turns highly unpromising raw materials that no-one would want into something that on a good day is quite splendid.

To induce second fermentation, you add a dose of sugar and yeast dissolved in wine to the bottle and close it with a crown cap. Some houses, as a mark of respect for their top wines, use wired cork closures for this process – worth looking out for during a visit. The bottles are stacked horizontally in the cellars on *lattes* (thin, wooden laths) and left, disturbed only by parties of tourists, to ferment once again.

The process takes longer than first fermentation because the temperature is cooler in the cellar. These days hardly any bottles burst, but most cellars will lose a couple; look out for jagged-edged gaps in the banks of bottles as you go by. Once second fermentation is over the wine sits on the dead lees and acquires more depth of flavour from the decomposing yeast cells. This is called autolysis. The longer you leave the bottle – it can be as long as five years – the richer and more complex the wine will be. Also, the longer you leave it the more you tie up your capital, so the more the bottle costs.

Next you remove the lees by *remuage* (riddling). These days the romantic sight of the troglodytic *remueur*, turning thousands of bottles a day as he progresses through the *pupitre*-filled cellars, is becoming rarer (although some big firms do employ one to keep the tourists happy). Even in smaller, artisans' cellars you're likely to see pallets of 500 bottles on Star Wars-like pods, called *gyropalettes* or *pupimatiques*, being shaken and turned en masse. Some of these are computer-controlled and run 24 hours a day, reducing a two or three month process to a week. Your host will debate the pros and cons of each method with you; those who still do it by hand will tell you the mechanical method is harmful in some way, the mechanists will tell you it's beneficial.

There's a good chance you'll see a disgorging line in action, as they run according to demand for most of the year. In most cases the process is mechanical, although in some small houses and for deluxe brands it may still be done by hand. The necks of the inverted bottles pass through a freezing brine solution, the crown cap is flipped off and the lees, frozen into a pellet of ice, shoot out with the force of a bullet. There's an inspection to make sure no debris is left in the bottle, then the wine is dosed with more sugar dissolved in wine (unless it's to be a totally dry champagne) and finally corked.

Get a good look a the cork; in its manufactured state it's completely cylindrical, so you can imagine the force exerted to get it into the bottle. A champagne cork is a composite of bits of cork, with two discs of better quality cork at the business end, nearest the wine. It will have the word 'champagne' stamped on it somewhere where it can't be tampered with once the cork is in the bottle. You may be given one as a souvenir.

A metal cap is fitted on top of the cork to prevent the wire cutting into it. The wine is then left to rest and to assimilate the sugar *dosage* evenly throughout itself; this can take up to another 18 months. Finally it's labelled. Non–vintage champagne must be at least three years old, vintage a minimum of five years old.

Much is made within the great champagne houses of the art and skill of the blender in mixing a set of harsh, raw, acidic young wines from three different grape varieties, and perhaps from all over the region, into the house style, something that people will recognize as being uniquely yours, year in year out. Everyone is making wine from the same grapes and the same vineyards. In order to make your brand stand out you have to emphasize the special character of your blend.

Unfortunately, this argument trips over something called the '*sur-lattes* scandal'. When champagne sales were booming, say in the late 1980s, some houses ran out of wine to sell. They thought nothing of buying in bottles from other suppliers '*sur-lattes*', from the maturing laths in someone else's cellars. The purchaser then simply slapped on his or her label and pushed them out. Now you're not going to have much influence over creating the unique house blend if you've bought in the wine as a finished product, are you?

The big champagne houses' attitude to blending is unique in French winemaking; their intention is to iron out any sense of where the wine has come from. The small-scale grower, on the other hand, can reflect local characteristics more directly. As you follow the wine route there are certainly opportunities to spot these different attributes. Discovering the growers is also one of the best reasons for visiting Champagne. Although they account for perhaps a third of all champagne produced, only about 7% of their wine is exported. The big houses dominate the export market, so getting out there yourself is the best way of discovering individual growers' wines.

HAS THE BUBBLE BURST?

A FEW WORDS ON VISITING CHAMPAGNE

Champagne is expensive. Huge price hikes at the beginning of the 1990s put a third of us off buying at home. Prices are beginning to come down, but not enough for me. Although the formula of buying at source for half the high street price just about applies, you can still buy New World sparklers in the UK for less than you'll pay per bottle in Reims or Epernay for the Grandes Marques. With the small-scale producers I recommend, however, you'll find champagnes that offer quality for your money way above that of the New World sparkling wines.

These producers are in most cases not the well-known names, but small- or medium-scale growers who have something special to offer. If you want to visit the glossy Grandes Marques by all means do so, remembering all the time that their multi-million pound investment in tourist facilities is paid for by you every time you buy their brand. Here you'll be treated like a tourist; there's nothing wrong with that, but you won't get close to the process or the people, and you <u>will</u> be treated to a large dose of the glamour-and-magic-of-champagne message, which I for one would rather avoid.

The Champenois are said to be worried about the decline in sales, and the fact that nearly a million bottles lie stockpiled in their cellars. (It's good news for us, though; the longer they languish, the better the wines will taste when sold.) They're also said to be worried about the decline in tourism, as fewer people leave the motorway to visit their region now the link to Burgundy is open. But if they are concerned, they're not showing it; hotel and restaurant prices are still steep. Money just doesn't seem to go as far in Champagne.

Nevertheless the region heaves with tourists from every part of Europe. It's particularly popular with the British as it's the first wine region we come across in France. Unlike the other regions I cover, most of the hotels and restaurants I recommend in Champagne are thoroughly 'discovered' by British tourists, although there are one or two that are new.

PLANNING THE ROUTE

Reims is the obvious starting-point as the motorway carves right through it. You can be there from Calais in two to three hours, depending on whether you observe the speed limit. (Please do. Brits are terribly conspicuous on this piece of road, and I know several who have been caught speeding.) From Ostend the journey is equally easy – you simply drop down via Lille.

Reims is a very useful stopover point for longer journeys to Alsace or Burgundy. There are a couple of hotels just five minutes from the motorway which are relatively easy to find. Ambonnay is close to the Epernay motorway exit, and Epernay itself is feasible for an overnight stop. (For hotels, see Listings pages 140–1.) It's even possible to add a 'mini-tour' of Champagne to your exploration of another region. As little as one day can allow you to visit some of the recommended producers and explore a stretch of the wine route – before heading on to better weather perhaps.

If you'd like to explore Champagne in more depth, however, you could consider up to a day in Reims, a day touring the route to Epernay, and a day in Epernay and covering points south or west. Then I'd suggest driving down to the Aube, where the scenery is very attractive, the tourists scarcer and the prices on the whole more affordable (see The Golden Triangle).

EXPLORING CHAMPAGNE

The starting point is **Reims**. Pronunciation first: the English way is 'Reams' whereas the French say 'Rams', preferably swallowing the 'm' in a nice, guttural, mid-throat snarl.

You can base yourself just outside if you're passing through. Near the motorway, on the outskirts of the city, is the Assiette Champenoise (take the Tinqueux exit from the A26 and then the N31 in the direction of Reims; it's on the left before a Mobil garage). This has large, comfortable rooms with brilliant beds, an indoor swimming-pool (in deference, no doubt, to the weather) and a Michelin-starred restaurant. The dining-room is very welcoming and attractive, with flocks of attentive staff. There's delicious lobster, but I must warn you about the chicken, which managed to be both tough and tasteless. These days many top chefs are absent from the stove half the year, so it was good to see the main man firmly in control (and at the bar once the meal was over). There's a vast buffet breakfast with exotic fruit salad and the like, and a very warm welcome from Madame, although the receptionist is fierce. The restaurant is very popular with the local business community, and the hotel with international tourists.

I don't usually recommend hotel chains, as I find them rather soulless and regimented, but the Campanile Sud, just outside Reims on the N51 Epernay road, is easy to find and has quiet rooms and a reasonably-priced, basic restaurant. (It's a British tour operator's base

CHAMPAGNE

▼ Wine producer
H Hotel
R Restaurant
See Listings pages 138–41
for further details

0   10   20 km

hotel.) Devotees of the shoe warehouse La Halle des Chaussures, purveyors of absurdly cheap footwear to the fascinated, like myself, will find a branch just around the corner.

Overlooking the motorway and the parallel Marne Canal is the Hôtel Liberté, complete with appropriate statue. Rooms are well-insulated from noise outside, and it's close to both the motorway and the city centre. It has a restaurant full of modern flavours, but I think you could do better elsewhere.

At Au Petit Comptoir, for instance, there's stylish bistro food under the auspices of the local Michelin three-star chef. Or try Le Vigneron, full of wine curiosities, with an interesting champagne-only wine list and hearty food. Au Petit Bacchus, in an atmospheric old wine building, offers good bistro food at prices much lower than the other two. For a quick steak-*frites*, look no further than the trio of restaurants all under the same management opposite the cathedral, Le Colibri, La Notre-Dame and Le Flamm'Steak.

The cathedral is well worth a visit, and meandering round adjacent streets will reveal plenty that is of architectural merit. Many champagne houses are based here and you can turn up at most of them on spec for a tour. The tourist information centre by the cathedral will give you a map which locates them.

The first visit in Reims I'd recommend, however, is quite unlike these grand tourist operations. In fact there are no winemaking processes to see and the company is so self-effacing that it hasn't even got an address plate outside. I suggest it for those who'd like to experience things done the old-fashioned way, and perhaps imagine they're a wine merchant for half an hour.

To visit **DELBECK** you first need to make an appointment through the firm's UK agent, Sam Gordon Clark of Onslow Pelham. He's happy to arrange everything for you. When you're admitted, you'll be taken into the boardroom and offered a glass of champagne to taste, and you'll have the opportunity to discuss business prospects with a senior member of staff (in immaculate English if required).

Delbeck was originally an old family firm, describing itself as 'Supplier to the former Court of France' and well known half a century ago. The name threatened to disappear, swallowed up in a series of take-overs, but a family company bought it and is re-establishing the firm. Eventually Delbeck will have cellars and a wine museum to show you, but for now just sit back in the elegant boardroom while you work out how many cases you can fit in the boot. The 1985 vintage (an excellent year, not much of which is left) costs FF115–150.

The Montagne de Reims wine route begins at Gueux, but at this point it's dull. If you're staying at the Assiette Champenoise, I'd pick it up at **Jouy-lès-Reims**. Otherwise leave Reims on the N51 to Epernay (passing the Campanile) and turn left onto the wine route, signposted Villers-Allerand and Rilly-la-Montagne, the D26. Luckily this route isn't shy of announcing itself: enormous signs proclaiming: 'Route Touristique de la Champagne' adorn every crossroads.

The road skirts the edge of the Montagne de Reims. Stop in quiet **Rilly-la-Montagne** and above the village square you'll find the house of **VILMART**. Founded in 1890, this family firm is now run by young Laurent Champs, who's taking over from his father. It's open for sales on spec, but make an appointment and Laurent will show you the cellars, with their use of wood. The Champs family is a great proponent of barrel fermentation, even forming a *confrérie* to celebrate it; Laurent's father was a cooper who married into wine. No fertilizer or weed-killer is used in the vineyard but, contrasting with traditional methods, they do use *gyropalettes* for riddling.

These are wines of exceptional quality and at remarkable prices: the NV is under FF80, but it's worth paying the extra for the prestige wines – up to FF112. This is amazingly good value for such high quality. Laurent Champs is highly committed and passionate about his wines and will take the trouble to explain his philosophy in more depth if you're interested. If you only visit one grower in Champagne, make it Vilmart.

Continue along the wine road, which offers attractive views across the plain towards Reims if it's not foggy. Look out for the windmill, an odd sight amid a sea of vines. The Montagne de Reims is a black grape area and the pretty village of **Verzenay** is renowned for its Pinot Noir, classed as Grand Cru. **MICHEL ARNOULD** owns 12ha of it. This is very much a family business – you're received in the living-room by Michel Arnould himself or, for a little English, his son Patrice. It's a friendly, homely reception and the wines are very good.

The strength of growers' champagne is its ability to reflect its origins more specifically. At this estate, for instance, you can taste the power-ful effect of a predominantly Pinot Noir wine, full and rich. They use some Chardonnay, which they don't grow – apparently you can swap up to 5% of your production with another grower; above 5% and you must call yourself a *négociant*. Prices range from FF67 to FF100.

The wine route now descends into **Ambonnay**, where I'd recom-mend the friendly Auberge St-Vincent. Bedrooms have been recently renovated, and the rustic dining-room offers good food with more or less authentic regional roots. Don't miss the unique Ceremony of the Car Parking. At about 7.15pm all the hotel guests are summoned to their cars by a knock on the door – you can hear them coming down the corridor. (One group of four adults, in separate rooms but travelling in one car, were all summoned to perform the Ceremony jointly and severally.) During the day you park on the pavement near the hotel but in the evening the proprietors have access to an enclosed parking area. Once guests are installed in their cars, a procession forms and proceeds sedately up the high street into this compound. Make sure one of you stays sober long enough to complete the formalities.

A couple of kilometres from Ambonnay, at **Bouzy**, is the estate of **ANDRÉ CLOUET**. This is another Pinot Noir-producing Grand Cru village, which also makes the aptly-named Bouzy Rouge. Clouet has very good wines, and the estate is also worth a visit for the little wine museum created in an old attic built centuries ago to house visiting grape-pickers.

Now if you speak French, no doubt you'll be received by the master of the house, Pierre Clouet. No problems there. If you ask for a visit in English, you'll meet his son Jean-François; and if you do, anything could happen. He may tell you he owns the estate; he may open a bottle for you to taste, or maybe not: 'I am not a café' (although he did go on to indicate that if you crossed his palm with silver, corks would fly); he may show you right round the estate. Alternatively he may be on another planet. The visit with Jean-François was, in truth, vastly entertaining; just take along a pinch of salt. His ambition, he says, is to have his photo in *The Times* and he keeps threatening to send his portfolio. I can't wait.

From Bouzy follow the D19 and join the D34 into Louvois. If you want to head back to Reims, follow the narrow D34 as it climbs the Montagne de Reims – a very pretty road. On the right, there's a signpost for the Faux de Verzy, a collection of strange, deformed beech trees, twisted like corkscrews. For the valiant, there's a path the other side of the road leading after an hour's walk to the Mont Sinai viewpoint, a First World War observation post. It's worthwhile only in good weather. You can then rejoin the wine road back to Reims (the D26).

Otherwise, take the D9 from Louvois to **Ay**, and visit **AYALA**. This house is a member of the Grandes Marques but doesn't proclaim itself as loudly as most. By appointment you can have an English-language tour and tasting of its light-bodied, delicate wines. Curious artefacts include an old, ornately-carved vat still used for allowing the wines to 'marry' between *assemblage* (blending) and bottling.

In the cellars, at the end of the rows, I noticed bright circles of light-bulbs. As I grew close I saw that there was only one light bulb, surrounded by a ring of reflectors like flower petals. I thought this was just an economy measure, but no. They're there for safety reasons. Cellar workers driving fork-lift trucks down endless cellar passage-ways can become mesmerized; when the 'sun' lights change pattern, they know they're getting near to the wall and must slow down.

From Ay head into **Epernay** and brace yourself for traffic jams (I'd advise parking as soon as you see a space, or following signposts for the vast Arcades underground car park – it's one of those where you have to pay a machine before joining the queue to get out). Epernay is home to some of the major names in champagne, such as Moët & Chandon, but I'd like to suggest visiting somewhere on a rather smaller scale: **ALFRED GRATIEN**.

This is a very traditional house and sister company of Gratien & Meyer (qv) in Saumur. It makes very serious champagne by time-honoured methods, including barrel fermentation. You can tour the cellars by appointment and see various old implements which were in use until surprisingly recently. These wines are highly respected within the wine trade but don't receive much publicity. I think they're worth discovering.

In Epernay you can stay at the Champagne and eat at another Petit Comptoir (the same set-up as in Reims) or in the Wine-Bar attached to the Hôtel Berceaux. The latter offers a wide selection of wines by the glass, and good-value dishes and set-price menus. Excellent regional cheeses for picnics are at Les Délices de la Ferme on Place des Arcades, while J M Corda on Rue Mercier has speciality breads and fine *pâtisserie*; also try Charcuterie de la Poste on Place Hugues Plomb.

If this marks the end of your tour, you can head home via Château-Thierry through the Vallée de la Marne. Keep to the north bank, on the D1, which is quieter than the N road on the south bank. Take the wine-route detours, clearly signposted, if you wish. After lunch in **Château-Thierry** (see Listings page 141) you can be in Calais for a late-afternoon ferry.

Alternatively, follow the wine route south of Epernay into the Côte des Blancs. Here Chardonnay predominates and the wines are lighter and more delicate. Visit the estate of **PIERRE PETERS** in **Le Mesnil-sur-Oger**. This is the first champagne grower I ever visited. It's a small operation producing very good wines, and you can tour the cellars with an English-speaking guide by appointment. Prices are very fair, too, with non-vintage from FF76 and vintage from FF96. There's also a good restaurant in the village, Le Mesnil.

The route now leads you through **Vertus**, where you can stay at the Hostellerie La Reine Blanche, which has an indoor swimming-pool and basic food; or the really brave can try the Mont-Aimé, in **Bergères-lès-Vertus**. I've stayed here twice, on visits separated by seven years, and in that time the welcome has gone from frosty to downright hostile. The food's deteriorated too. Why am I suggesting you stay here? Well, the rooms are comfortable and good value, and there's a pool. Perhaps this is the venue for a sneaky picnic to compensate for earlier overeating. That's what I did, anyway.

After this you could follow the wine route on to Sézanne, but I wouldn't recommend it. The scenery is dull and so is Sézanne, although the local cooperative, **LE BRUN DE NEUVILLE**, does offer very good quality wines at reasonable prices and a chance to see a major operation in action. (To reach it, follow the signs in **Bethon** for Chantemerle.)

Instead, I'd recommend heading on down the motorway to the Champagne section of The Golden Triangle, the Aube, to see if you think the bigwigs in Reims are right to look down their noses at it.

Listings

When telephoning France from the UK, the number must be preceded by the digits 010 33. Producers are listed in wine route order, and hotels/restaurants by town or village according to the route. Accommodation prices are per room, meal prices are per head.

Producers

Delbeck
51067 Reims
To make an appointment, contact UK agent Sam Gordon Clark at Onslow Pelham & Co, 23 South Terrace, London SW7 2JB, Tel 071 584 5420, Fax 071 225 1006
Credit cards accepted
Good English

Vilmart & Cie
5 rue des Gravières (Place de la Mairie), 51500 Rilly-la-Montagne
Tel 26 03 40 01, Fax 26 03 46 57
Open Mon–Fri 8.30–12, 14–18;
Nov & Dec also open Sat;
visits by appointment to cellar
Credit cards accepted
Good English

Michel Arnould
28 rue de Mailly, 51360 Verzenay
Tel 26 49 40 06, Fax 26 49 44 61
Open Mon–Fri 9–12, 14–18;
visits by appointment Sat & Sun
Some English

André Clouet
8 rue Gambetta, 51150 Bouzy
Tel 26 57 00 82
Visits by appointment
Good English

Ayala
2 boulevard du Nord, 51160 Ay
Tel 26 55 15 44, Fax 26 51 09 04
Visits by appointment Mon–Fri;
also Sat & Sun during harvest
Credit cards accepted
Some English (by appointment)

Alfred Gratien
30 rue Maurice-Cerveaux, BP 3, 51201 Epernay
Tel 26 54 38 20, Fax 41 51 03 55
Visits by appointment
Some English

Pierre Peters
26 rue des Lombards,
51190 Le Mesnil-sur-Oger
Tel 26 57 50 32, Fax 26 57 97 71
Open Mon–Sat 9–12, 14–18
Credit cards accepted
Some English (by appointment)

Le Brun de Neuville
Route de Chantemerle,
51260 Bethon
Tel 26 80 48 43, Fax 26 80 43 28
Visits by appointment Mon–Sat 8–12, 14–18 (by arrangement with M di Florio)
Credit cards accepted
Some English

GRANDES MARQUES

The following is a selection of big champagne houses which I believe are worth visiting, either because they offer an interesting tour or because the wines are good – although the two may coincide. There may be an entrance fee (typically FF20–40), for which you usually get a glass of champagne and perhaps something special like a miniature train to save you the effort of walking round the cellars. Treat the visit as you would any tourist attraction – you'll get something for your money, the champagne will be cheaper here than in a bar, and the entrance fee absolves you from any obligation to buy. It's always worth making a quick phone call in advance, to confirm arrangements, even if an appointment isn't mandatory. I would be very surprised if any of these houses could not answer you in English.

Reims

Piper-Heidsieck
51 boulevard Henri-Vasnier,
51100 Reims
Tel 26 84 41 94
Ride the *circuit de visite*, a hugely expensive installation – not a train, more a series of individual cars passing through various exhibits including outsize bunches of grapes.

Pommery
5 place du Général Gouraud,
51100 Reims
Tel 26 61 62 63
Mock Scottish baronial exterior, very elegant surroundings, enormous wall-carvings, rather like the Cheddar caves turned into a stately home; plenty of glamorous hostesses, and vast, recently-refurbished visitors' areas. Watch out for the descent into the cellars or, more to the point, the ascent out of them: you're climbing a staircase from a depth of 30m below ground.

Louis Roederer
21 boulevard Lundy, 51053 Reims
Tel 26 40 42 11
You must make an appointment to visit. Brilliant champagne; Cristal retails in the UK for £60-odd.

Epernay

De Castellane
57 rue de Verdun, 51204 Epernay
Tel 26 55 15 33
Plenty to see here: various museums (including one showing ancient means of champagne production), posters, a vast collection of labels and, for an extra charge, a heated butterfly garden (closed in winter). There's also a tower with a panoramic view.

Mercier
75 avenue de Champagne,
51333 Epernay
Tel 26 54 75 26
An all-singing, all-dancing tour, with audio-visual show, glass lifts, laser light show, train ride through the cellars, wall sculptures and the largest champagne cask ever made. The wine? Hmm...

Moët & Chandon
20 avenue de Champagne,
51333 Epernay
Tel 26 54 71 11
The largest champagne house and the one receiving the most visitors. Very well organized tours.

Perrier-Jouët
28 avenue de Champagne,
51200 Epernay
Tel 26 55 20 53
You must make an appointment to visit. See the Maison Belle Epoque with its splendid collection of art nouveau furniture. Lovely wines, and the most beautiful champagne bottle, the Belle Epoque.

Ay
Bollinger
16 rue Jules Lobet, 51160 Ay
Tel 26 55 21 31
Bollinger recently produced a Charter of Ethics and Quality, the first Grande Marque to do so, with the implication that the great houses should take a lead in improving standards in the champagne trade. These are some of the best champagnes, with prices to match.

Avize
Bricout
Ancien Château d'Avize,
29 Rempart du Midi, 51160 Ay
Tel 26 57 53 93
Brought to fame by our dear departed Chancellor, Bricout is a better wine than the 'cheap champagne' the tabloids claim he bought. The château is very attractive.

Hotels and Restaurants
H Hotel   *R* Restaurant

Reims
HR L'Assiette Champenoise
40 avenue P-Vaillant-Couturier,
51430 Tinqueux
Tel 26 04 15 56, Fax 26 04 15 69
Rooms FF500–785, Meals FF350–500
(member of Relais du Silence)

HR Campanile Sud
Avenue Georges Pompidou,
Val-de-Murigny, 51100 Reims
Tel 26 36 66 94, Fax 26 49 95 40
Rooms FF268, Meals FF80–102

HR Hôtel Liberté
55 rue Boulard, 51100 Reims
Tel 26 40 52 61, Fax 26 47 27 38
Rooms FF390–420, Meals FF155–370

R Au Petit Bacchus
11 rue Université
Tel 26 47 10 05
FF60–150

R Au Petit Comptoir
17 rue Mars
Tel 26 40 58 58
FF150–220

R Le Vigneron
Place P Jarnot
Tel 26 47 00 71
FF155

Ambonnay
HR Auberge St-Vincent
Rue St-Vincent,
51150 Ambonnay
Tel 26 57 01 98, Fax 47 57 32 50
Rooms FF290–360, Meals FF120–350

Epernay
H Champagne
30 rue E Mercier, 51200 Epernay
Tel 26 55 30 22, Fax 26 51 94 63
FF255–390

R Au Petit Comptoir
3 rue Dr Rousseau
Tel 26 51 53 53
FF160–225

R Wine-Bar
13 rue de Berceaux
Tel 26 55 28 84
FF60–120
(The Hôtel Berceaux, to which this restaurant is attached, is under new management and standards may change.)

Le Mesnil-sur-Oger
R Le Mesnil
2 rue Pasteur
Tel 26 57 95 57
FF100–350

Vertus
HR Hostellerie La Reine Blanche
18 avenue L Lenoir, 51130 Vertus
Tel 26 52 20 76, Fax 26 52 16 59
Rooms FF395–430, Meals FF135–290

Bergères-lès-Vertus
HR Le Mont-Aimé
4–6 rue Vertus,
51130 Bergères-lès-Vertus
Tel 26 52 21 31, Fax 26 52 21 39
Rooms FF230–410, Meals FF100–350

Château-Thierry and Domptin
R Auberge Jean de la Fontaine
10 rue Filoirs, Château-Thierry
Tel 23 83 63 89
FF120–350

R Le Cygne d'Argent
Domptin (8km southeast of Château-Thierry)
Tel 23 70 43 11
FF66–325

Alsace

Alsace was the first French wine region I ever visited and it remains one of my favourites. The scenery is heartstopping, the hospitality warm and unforced, the wines as inviting as the people. Stuck away in the northeastern corner of France, it receives few British visitors, yet it's perfect territory for buying direct from the grower.

Alsace's recent history has been marked by war and upheaval: annexed by Germany after the Franco-Prussian war, in 1870, it was returned to France after the First World War only to be occupied by the Nazis in 1940.

Under the Germans both the French language and the local dialect, known as Elsässisch or Alsacien, were banned. Relations are now happily more cordial, as the number of German weekend tourists shows. (Book weekend accommodation about a fortnight in advance.) Alsace is also a popular destination for Scandinavian wine buyers, suffering as they do from wine taxation laws of an idiocy comparable to our own.

Both the architecture and the cuisine are marked by similarities to the other side of the Rhine, but the Germanic ingredients are tempered by the elegance and finesse of French culinary tradition. The wines, too, use some grape varieties thought of as German, such as Riesling, but the winemaking style has a definite French accent.

Alsace forms a long, thin north–south strip, with the winemaking area sandwiched to the west by the Vosges mountains and to the east by the fertile agricultural plain alongside the Rhine. The Vosges trap most of the rainfall that plagues the rest of northern France. Alsace receives just a quarter of the rain which falls on land west of the hills, making Colmar the second driest town in the country. Add good sunshine, especially in late summer and autumn, and you get potentially excellent conditions both for grape harvesting and for tourism.

The explorer in Alsace will discover one of the prettiest wine regions imaginable. The heart of the wine road takes you through a succession of villages all competing with each other for one of the 'village in bloom' awards, geraniums cascading out of window-boxes at every turn, tubs of flowers in the village square. Except for those villages bombed to bits during the Second World War, the narrow streets and ancient buildings are intact and well cared for. There are several tourist honeypots that are remarkably attractive – and popular – but there are many more which, while not being quite so chocolate-box, have much charm with the added bonus of being places where people can actually live and work without feeling on daily display.

In many parts of the region the local dialect is still widely spoken. This has strong links with the German dialects still heard on the other side of the Rhine, and as a German speaker I can just about make sense of it, although it's absorbing more and more French words. A generation ago it was the first language children spoke. The local English teacher in Itterswiller, now 53, told me he didn't learn a word of French until he went to school at the age of seven. Sadly, like many local languages, it is fading out because children no longer learn it at home.

When to visit? All year round, of course, but I've found Alsace a particularly comforting place to be in the autumn and winter. The foliage is beautiful as it turns gold, the air is full of the smell of wood-smoke, the geraniums flower well into November. (It can get very cold, so do bring thermals.) In the weeks before Christmas there are markets in several villages, notably Kaysersberg, where traditional decorations, wooden toys and craft-work are on sale, and the festive illuminations look magical at dusk. The light across the mountains at this time of year can be stunning. Occasionally there's fog, but if this descends while you're there, take a road into the mountains and, at perhaps 600m, the air will suddenly clear and you'll emerge into brilliant sunshine while all below you is miserable.

HOW THE WINES ARE CLASSIFIED

Basic Alsace wine law is simple, although over the last decade or so several steps have been taken to make it more complicated. At the root of it all is the grape variety. Alsace used varietal labelling long before it became fashionable, and the grapes are still the key to understanding the wines. There are eight grape names you'll encounter: Riesling, Tokay Pinot Gris, Gewurztraminer, Muscat, Pinot Blanc, Pinot Noir, Sylvaner and Chasselas. The situation does get a little hazy with the Pinots: Pinot Blanc wine can also be made from the Pinot Auxerrois grape (although one or two winemakers swear these two taste quite different and are happy to demonstrate this to you in the glass). It can even be made from Pinot Noir vinified white, or from Pinot Gris (goodness knows why).

So far, so reasonably simple. But some vineyard sites are better than others and so a system of naming Grand Cru vineyards was instigated in the 1980s. There are now 50 and, as you can imagine, much politicking surrounds which vineyards are 'in' and which 'out'.

Grand Cru wines have more stringent regulations all round. For ordinary AC Alsace, a minimum of just 8.5% alcohol is required and a hectare of vines is allowed to produce a maximum of 100hl of juice. This permitted yield is much lower for Grand Cru wines and the minimum level of alcohol is higher. Only certain noble grape varieties can become Grand Cru wine in the first place (Riesling, Gewurztraminer, Pinot Gris, Pinot Noir and Muscat) but not all of these are necessarily permitted in a particular Grand Cru vineyard. Other varieties may also be planted on these sites but you can't say on the label that they've been grown in a Grand Cru vineyard. There are, however, various ingenious ways of getting round this, such as putting the initial of the Grand Cru site on the label.

Top of the range of Alsace wines are *vendange tardive*, from late-harvested grapes, and *sélection des grains nobles*, from individually selected grapes affected by noble rot (see page 56). You can find these made from Riesling, Gewurztraminer, Pinot Gris and Muscat. They have high potential alcohol and are the finest and dearest of Alsace's wines.

In addition to these official designations, individual producers, as elsewhere in France, have ways of letting you know which of their wines they consider better (and therefore charge more for). They may call them *réserve* or *cuvée spéciale*, or give them special brand names. It's also permissible to name certain vineyards on the label even if they're not official Grand Cru sites. The Kaefferkopf vineyard in Ammerschwihr is a well-known example of these *lieux-dits*, or 'named places' (and I gather there was some serious politicking about its status going on recently). Most price lists will show a clear progression from the basic AC Alsace wine, identified only by grape variety, through some fancy names, up to Grand Cru sites, perhaps with a *vendange tardive* to finish off the list.

Alsace shows how wine laws haven't existed immutably for centuries but are constantly evolving and changing. The regulations here were only initiated after 1945 and are still being revised. There's even a call for a level of Premier Cru to sit somewhere between the generic wines and the Grands Crus. There's nothing like making a situation even more complicated, is there?

Alsace winemakers usually offer most of the permitted grape varieties, at several quality levels and often from several vintages. The cheaper, generic wines are best drunk while young and fresh (the wines, that is), within a year or two of the vintage. Dearer wines and Grands Crus can often be drunk young, or after a gap of a few years of dumb adolescence during which they're not worth touching. Producers are only too happy to suggest how long a wine will take to mature.

WHAT YOU'LL SEE IN THE CELLAR

Grapes are the key to understanding Alsace's wines, so a brief description of each of the main varieties and their wines seems to be in order.

Riesling This is a high acidity wine. In youth fruity and refreshing, with age it acquires an oily smell of petrol, is often minerally and is very rich and elegant in the mouth. Sometimes when you taste a young Grand Cru Riesling it will hit you with its lush fruit straight away; sometimes it can seem rather thin and insignificant, and you will wonder what all the fuss (and price) is about. The Grands Crus can age for a decade or more and often need several years' patience before they start to show you what they've got.

Tokay Pinot Gris Locally, Pinot Gris has long been known as Tokay, but Eurocrats have tried to ban the name, arguing that the consumer could confuse it with Hungarian Tokay. Alsace winemakers have had no truck with this regulation, nor with the compromise suggestion that the wine should be called Tokay Pinot Gris d'Alsace. Expect any variation of the above names, in any order. The wine is a little lower in acidity than Riesling, with a spicy nose when well made and a rich, full-bodied taste. Alsaciens like it with food. It's not widely grown, accounting for only about 5% of plantings, but is becoming popular with Parisiens, which explains the increase in price.

Gewurztraminer 'Gewürz' means 'spicy' in German (the umlaut is dropped in Alsace), but the smell of this grape is more like ripe exotic fruit, such as lychees, highly perfumed flowers, like overblown roses or elderflowers, or even turkish delight. It can have high alcohol content with low acidity, and although it has a blowsy, sweet nose it is fermented dry (except for some exceptional *sélection des grains nobles*). As you move along the wine route you may be struck by the variation in styles of Gewurztraminer, from blowsy, fat opulent wines to restrained, more subtle examples. These are created partly by the difference in soils and partly by the varying attitudes of the winemakers.

Muscat This wine comes as a surprise to anyone who knows the sweet Muscats of southern France and elsewhere since, like all Alsace wines, it is dry. The nose is aromatic, grapey and floral, and seems sweet, but the wine is dry and fruity in the mouth and makes a wonderful aperitif.

Pinot Blanc, Pinot Auxerrois, Clevner/Klevner ...grouped all together. Pinot Auxerrois is a relation of Pinot Blanc, slightly spicier in taste but often blended anonymously with its cousin. As mentioned earlier, some producers, such as Rolly Gassmann (qv), make separate wines from both and advanced students might enjoy comparing the two. Clevner/Klevner is a term specific to Alsace and refers to a wine made from a Pinot variety. This wine is definitely for drinking young. Klevner de Heiligenstein, on the other hand, isn't a Pinot at all but a form of the Savagnin grape, related to Gewurztraminer. It's only grown in small quantities, around Heiligenstein. Taste it at Klipfel (qv). Both this and the Pinot Blanc grape are fresh, fruity and fairly neutral.

Pinot Noir The great red grape of Burgundy generally metamorphoses into a rosé wine in Alsace. So far north, it's difficult to get the grapes ripe enough to extract sufficient colour and tannin to make a decent red. But there are exceptions, notably at Zind-Humbrecht (qv), where they can offer an elegant red wine of great finesse and character (at a price). Most places, however, will offer you a deep pink wine, with an attractive smell and taste of creamy, ripe fruit and good acidity, which goes surprisingly well with red meats.

Sylvaner Not a complex wine: light and fruity, not much of a nose, best drunk young. Some producers lavish TLC on it to produce something more complex and interesting, but such wines are rare. It has low alcohol and refreshing acidity, making it a popular café 'quaffing' wine. It tends to be grown in the less favoured sites, particularly in the north, and is in decline (although still accounting for nearly 20% of plantings).

Edelzwicker This is a blend of noble and less noble varieties, in most cases Sylvaner, Pinot Blanc, Auxerrois and Chasselas (a rather dull grape not usually sold as a varietal wine and declining rapidly in planted area). It's cheap and cheerful and to be drunk as young as possible.

Crémant d'Alsace The region's sparkling wine *appellation* is made by the champagne – sorry, traditional – method, involving second fermentation in bottle and a minimum of nine months on the lees (although look out for better wines, which are left on their lees for longer; 12–24 months' contact with the spent yeasts imparts more flavour to the wine, which is helpful when it's made from a neutral grape variety such as Pinot Blanc). Crémant d'Alsace has been an AC wine only since 1976, but the rules for production are nearly as stringent as those for champagne itself. It has grown hugely in popularity, now selling over 10M bottles a year, and some is very good indeed – a creditable alternative to champagne at under half the price. Don't be put off by the fizzy, one-dimensional examples that find their way into many British wine shops. When you've discovered a producer you like, try his or her Crémant – you may find a real bargain.

Where the grapes are grown is particularly significant, too. I doubt if there's anywhere else in France where so many soil types occur in such a small area – the result of the same volcanic activity that created the Alps. Each grape variety responds differently to these soils and some growers love to study the effect this has on the taste of their wines. If you don't think the *terroir* can influence the taste, come to Alsace. There are winemakers here who will delight in spending several hours explaining the intricacies to you, illustrated with tasting-samples.

PLANNING THE ROUTE

The most straightforward route is via the Calais ferries or the Channel Tunnel; direct on the motorway, and with a very early crossing and an iron will, you can be in Strasbourg by teatime. (Calais to Strasbourg is 630km.) Lesser mortals may prefer to break the journey in Champagne, which is reachable from Calais in under three hours (see Champagne pages 130–2 for hotels near the motorway). The motorway toll from Calais to Reims is FF86, and from Reims to Strasbourg FF115.

One way of avoiding the tolls, especially for those based north of Watford, is to take a ferry from Hull or Felixstowe landing at Zeebrugge, and to take the A10 to Brussels and Luxembourg, dropping down via the A4 and A31 to join the A26 at Metz. This is a very practical route, slightly shorter than going via Calais, and brings the northern French wine areas within realistic striking distance of the north of England and Scotland. Travelling via Luxembourg also has the advantage of taking you to the cheapest petrol in northern Europe.

If you live close to the 'Loire' crossings via Portsmouth or Southampton then you may prefer to exchange one dire capital orbital motorway for another and to drive from Le Havre via Paris. From the Newhaven–Dieppe crossing there's a cross-country route to Alsace via Amiens and Reims, which is time-consuming but worth considering if time is not of the essence.

N

Strasbourg *H R*

Obernai

Ottrott

Mont-Ste-Odile

D35

Barr ♥

Andlau
H R

Itterswiller *H R* ● Epfig ♥

N83

Dambach-la-Ville

SÉLESTAT *H R*

St-Hippolyte
H R ♥

Thannenkirch *H R*
Rorschwihr ♥
Ribeauvillé *R* Bergheim *R* ♥

N83

Riquewihr
♥ Zellenberg
H R ♥

Kientzheim *H* ♥

Ammerschwihr
H R ♥
Turckheim ♥

A35

COLMAR *H R* ♥

Wintzenheim ♥

Eguisheim *R*

Husseren-les-
Châteaux ♥

N83 ↓ Mulhouse

Westhalten
H R ♥

ALSACE

♥ Wine producer
H Hotel
R Restaurant
See Listings pages 168–71
for further details

0   10   20 km

EXPLORING ALSACE

The Alsace wine road is about 200km long, zigzagging from north of Strasbourg down to Thann near Mulhouse. As with all wine roads, the choice of route is dictated by local politics and just because a village is on the wine route doesn't mean it's worth stopping there. To my mind, the central section of the route is most worthy of your attention. When you get to the end, all you can reasonably do is turn around and come back again, but it won't seem repetitive. First of all, the scenery looks completely different from the other direction. Secondly, you can divert from the wine route to follow one of the other waymarked routes, such as the Route des Crêtes, which leads you up into stunning hairpin-bend hills and great views. Incidentally, Alsace is pretty hot on fancy routes; latest additions include the Route of the Fried Pike-Perch and the Route of Fermented Cabbage.

Thirdly, this is a badly signposted route and if my experience is anything to go by you'll find yourself off course with depressing ease. This route doesn't believe in anything so useful as signposts at junctions or roundabouts; all it will do, most of the time, is put up little signs beneath the ones you see at the entry to a village, confirming in irritatingly small print that you are indeed still on the right road – very helpful. Happily the route's zigzag nature means that when you get lost, probably all you've done is missed out a dog-leg and arrived at the next town but one, so when you turn around and head north you can pick up any places you inadvertently missed going south. Most of the time my suggested route follows the official one but there are some points where the route disappears or is simply uninteresting, and in these cases I've offered alternatives.

Although we think of Alsace as one region, politically it is divided into two, with Bas-Rhin in the north and Haut-Rhin in the south. Once upon a time the two regions ignored each other to such an extent that they didn't even produce a joint map of the region; luckily the two tourist boards now speak to each other.

The southerly region accounts for nearly all the best wine. The Bas-Rhin has coarser soil and flatter vineyards, the Haut-Rhin has the classic sloping sites and correspondingly more beautiful scenery. As you head south, you can follow the development of wine styles, although of course you can't simply say that the wine improves as you move south; there are too many dedicated producers north of Sélestat dying to contradict this theory, some of whom are mentioned below.

In a region where over 65% of winemakers own less than a hectare and treat winemaking as a weekend hobby, you'll see forests of *vente directe* signs that signal properties that are simply too small to register in most guidebooks. If a property takes your fancy, check it out. Meanwhile, those producers I recommend make good wines, are happy to receive visitors and in most cases speak English.

Two obvious places to head for as a first-night stop are **Strasbourg** and La Petite-Pierre. Your choice depends to a certain extent on how you feel about navigating in towns. Strasbourg is certainly not for the faint-hearted, particularly since it has dug up most of its city centre to lay tramlines.

The hotel I would currently suggest there, the Sofitel, is large and corporate, but it's relatively easy to find without getting caught up in the roadworks and you can reach the major tourist attractions from it on foot. I've also enjoyed staying at the Hôtel des Rohan, opposite the cathedral (an austere and beautiful building with an amazingly complex astronomical clock which goes into action at 12.30pm every day; be there by 12.15 or they won't let you in). Petite-France, a pedestrianized area of ancient, half-timbered buildings including the Tanners' Quarter, offers attractive walks.

There are several highly-rated restaurants, but I prefer to eat at one of the *winstubs* or at Maison Kammerzell. *Winstubs* offer you good-value, authentic Alsace specialities in traditional surroundings, and I like them immensely. Try S'Burjerstuewel (Chez Yvonne) or

Zum Strissel. There are several excellent butchers/*charcuteries* where you can stock up on picnic goods – notably Frick-Lutz on Rue des Orfèvres, Kirn on Rue du 22-novembre, and Klein on Boulevard d'Anvers – and the homesick can buy BLT sandwiches from Marks et Spencer.

The countryside option is a stopover at **La Petite-Pierre**, near the Sarre-Union junction of the A4. This is a pretty mountain village with wonderful views. I must admit it's very much a tourist honey-pot, so you will be sharing your mountain idyll with half of Europe, but it's popular for a reason. There are several good tourist hotels in the centre, such as the Trois Roses, and one, the Auberge d'Imsthal, outside the village on the D178.

If you've stayed one night in Champagne en route, you might consider a lunch-time stop on your second day at La Grange du Paysan at **Hinsingen** (take the Sarreguemines exit off the A4 from Reims). But I should mention that if you eat here, the food comes in such huge portions that you would be wise to avoid Strasbourg's finest in the evening.

This was one of the first restaurants I visited in France and it remains a benchmark for honest, unpretentious regional cooking, brilliantly done. When I lived in Frankfurt it was somewhere to go for Sunday lunch, when they serve whole roast suckling pig. Before being carved it's paraded around the dining-room on a platter, to a round of applause. I can also warmly recommend their *pot-au-feu* (inadequately translated as 'stew'). Between the starter and the main course they serve *flammekueche*, a bacon, onion and cream-cheese tart on a wafer-thin dough base. Each table has a whole tart and you are given every encouragement to finish it.

The route proper starts at Marlenheim, but I'd recommend skipping the outer section and suggest you pick it up at **Ottrott** or **Obernai**. Almost at once you can deviate from it and climb to Mont-Ste-Odile, for ancient religious monuments and exceptional views (unless like me you visit when it's misty). Back on the road, **Barr** is the first stop for a producer and we begin on the nursery slopes.

DOMAINE KLIPFEL is right on the wine route, in the town, and is an easy place to visit. There's always someone on hand to welcome you in English, tasting is free and there's even an introductory slide show with English voice-over. And yes, there are drawbacks. The estate is heavily geared up for group visits and focusses on these rather than individual customers. Groups are served meals, for instance, which aren't available to individuals. You can visit the cellars and winemaking museum, a few streets away, but only during the week – it's parties only at the weekend. The chances are that you won't make direct contact with the winemaker here, but it's a straightforward place to visit, to ease you in perhaps, and the welcome is genuine. The wines are of a good standard and this is one of the few places to offer the local speciality, Klevner de Heiligenstein.

Nearby, reached via Mittelbergheim, is **Andlau**, a pretty village surrounded by steep slopes. Its abbey is currently undergoing extensive renovation. In the crypt is an ancient fertility symbol; local legend has it that if women sit on the back of the statue of the she-bear they will be pregnant within a year. Me, I wouldn't go near it.

The family that runs **DOMAINE GRESSER** has been living in the same house since 1667 and the present incumbent, 36-year-old Rémy Gresser, is a firm believer in passing on the land to future generations in as good a condition as he received it from his father. To this end he is a keen advocate of organic methods in the vineyard and has recently had great success in pest control using parasitic wasps. He welcomes visitors in a small, rustic-style tasting-room but is currently renovating a larger room which will offer more facilities. He's very committed to supporting Andlau and helps organize two- or three-day visits for people who want to explore this underrated area in more depth.

A full range of wines is offered; I was particularly impressed by the Rieslings, ranging from '92 generic at FF26 to various Grands Crus at FF56–70. Rémy Gresser owns several parcels of land on different soils and can take you through the effects of the *terroirs* on the taste of his wines – a first-class, dedicated producer, highly recommended.

The place to stay in the village is the Zinck-Hôtel. This is a design victim's dream. The hotel has been converted from an old mill and the workings can still be seen in the breakfast-room. Each room is individually designed, some on traditional lines, others decidedly eccentric. The most popular of these are called Jazzy, Branchée (switched-on) and Baroque. This last has emerald-green walls, a canopied bed covered in red brocade, and a sofa with claw feet that look like they're made from giant blue pipecleaners. It almost seems a shame to open your suitcase and spoil the designer lines by littering your underwear about. This place is a lot of fun. There's no restaurant, but the owner's brother runs a lively *winstub* in the village, Le Relais de la Poste. For grander meals try Au Boeuf Rouge. M Zinck is fascinating on local history; between him and Rémy Gresser you can really get information.

Leaving Andlau, heading south, the road climbs to give spectacular views. It passes through **Itterswiller**, a large, floral, touristy village well served with hotels and restaurants along the long main street. Fans of more traditional places to stay will prefer the rustic style of Hôtel Arnold. Some rooms have balconies and good views across the vineyards, and meals are served in a *winstub* close by. The ceiling in its panelled dining-room appears to be held up by giant winepress screws.

One table in the restaurant was occupied by a session of the local council on the night I was there. Debates were held in Elsässisch, the minutes written in French. The food has a heavy regional emphasis and is very good indeed: melting, unctuous *baeckeoffe* (a hearty stew), excellent *foie gras*, chicken with *spaetzle* (noodles). House wines are made by their own domaine and are on sale in a boutique next door. This also offers regional craft-work and tableware, attractively presented, as well as the home-made jam the hotel serves at breakfast.

Advanced students would be advised to deviate slightly from the wine road here and head to **Epfig**. **DOMAINE OSTERTAG** is run by André Ostertag and his sister. He identifies 70 distinct areas within his 10ha of vines and produces about 15 wines reflecting the effect of different soils on a number of grape varieties. If exploring this question in depth appeals to you then he's your man, and will give generously of his time, but he's not keen on starting from scratch.

He concentrates on Riesling, Pinot Gris and Gewurztraminer, and makes two ranges. One, in green bottles with green-lettered labels, emphasizes the taste of the grape; the other, with brown bottles and labels, emphasizes the effect of the soil. 'Wine for us is a reflection of our soil and our soul', he says. M Ostertag studied in Burgundy and this influences his technique: he makes Pinot Blanc in oak and uses *battonage* (stirs up the lees) every few days.

This is very personal winemaking. He hates the blowsy, overblown character many winemakers give Gewurztraminer and battles to restrain the grape's natural tendencies: 'I always fight against the grape. It's too exuberant. It's not the way I think you have to be in life'. Certainly he is himself restrained yet intense, lean and wiry; here is a classic example of the wine being an expression of the man. If you usually don't like Gewurztraminer, try his. You could be on to something.

The walled village of Dambach-la-Ville is worth exploring en route to **St-Hippolyte** (continue along the D35 and then join the D1B). St-Hippolyte is the first village of note in the Haut-Rhin and home to the estate of **KLEIN AUX VIEUX REMPARTS**. Françoise Klein and her husband farm 7ha of vines. She's particularly interested in the marriage of food and wine, and receives you in a pretty tasting-room where you can compare different vintages and the effect of her three vineyard soils: sand, limestone and granite. They specialize in Riesling Schlossreben, Gewurztraminer Schlossreben and Tokay Geisberg. (These aren't Grands Crus but named sites, *lieux-dits*.)

Unusually, the Kleins can offer vintages dating back to the mid-1980s, in their *vendanges tardives*. Priced at over FF100 a bottle, these are not cheap but the opportunity to taste such wines is rare. At the other end of the scale, their basic varietal range starts at just FF22. Also try the local speciality, Rouge de St-Hippolyte, aged in wood. Mme Klein is very warm and a fund of knowledge, as you might guess from the way she describes herself as 'winemaker-oenologist'. If you already have some experience of Alsace wines, she'll be particularly illuminating.

There are various options for an overnight stay. In St-Hippolyte itself is the Ducs de Lorraine, a classic Logis with a large dining-room with firmly-starched linen, candelabra, and traditional dishes, some more successful than others. Madame keeps a close eye on all stages of the meal and is most concerned that all should be well. Bedrooms are a mixture of classic and rustic in style. Many have balconies with good views across the village and up to the Haut-Koenigsberg which towers above it. Two rival churches chime the quarters right through the night. It's a British tour operator's base hotel; their clients have voted it the company's most welcoming.

Sélestat (signposted off the D201) is a medium-sized town nearby with one of Alsace's most beautiful Romanesque churches, the Eglise St-Foy, and the remarkable Humanist Library. For a little luxury, stay at the Hostellerie de l'Abbaye La Pommeraie, a recently-restored abbey in the town centre. Rooms are large and dramatically decorated, some Empire, all chandeliers and gilt, others Alsacien, with light wood panelling and imaginative upholstery. Sumptuous breakfasts provide enough for two meals. I think the restaurant is overreaching itself at present and the brasserie, offering simpler regional dishes, is probably a better bet. There's a warm, unstuffy welcome and a parting gift of *kugelhopf* cake.

If you'd like to move off the wine road and into the mountains, head for Auberge La Meunière in **Thannenkirch**. This village has an Alpine feel, with wonderful valley views. The rustic, panelled dining-room shares these views and offers good cooking: pork medallions in beer, beef with marrow and pickled shallots. Here for the first time I was offered bleeding chunks of meat as an *amuse-gueule* (like a mini-kebab, complete with sliver of green pepper). Rooms are modest and heavily-furnished; the most favoured have that view.

From the St-Hippolyte–Thannenkirch road it's just a few kilometres to Haut-Koenigsbourg, a splendid mountain viewpoint with a château to visit. Then descend from Thannenkirch to **Bergheim**. There's an excellent restaurant here, the Wistub du Sommelier. This is where I first tackled *choucroute* (sauerkraut) and it's also an ideal place to try other classic Alsace dishes at very reasonable prices. It has a good wine list.

Fortified, head back up the wine route a kilometre or so to **Rorschwihr** and **ROLLY GASSMANN**. No English is spoken here; it's a perfect example of how far you can get with smiles, nods and goodwill, and whatever you can manage in French or German. Louis and Marie-Thérèse (whose maiden name was Rolly) come from winemaking families dating back to 1676. These people are relaxed and happy, and so are their wines.

Even the most humble of varieties, Sylvaner, is full and round with surprising concentration for just FF25. Here you can taste the difference between Pinot Blanc and Auxerrois. This is user-friendly winemaking, where the philosophy is simplicity: 'The less you touch the grape, the better the wine will be'. I tasted their entire range on sale, 30 wines, and there wasn't one I wouldn't happily have bought – good stuff!

Return to Bergheim for a complete contrast, at **MARCEL DEISS**. If the Rolly Gassmanns and their wines are big and open-hearted, M & Mme Deiss are nervy and intense. And, unsurprisingly, so are their wines. Jean-Michel is in charge of the vineyards, his wife Clarisse is in charge of sales.

She has elevated direct-to-customer sales into an art, establishing early on what style of wine you prefer by assessing your response to two vintages of Muscat, and pitching her explanation of the estate according to how much you know about the wines and how much you want to spend. This is very helpful as the tasting is closely tailored to your requirements, and she'll give you all the time you need. Sometimes Mme Deiss may appear rather didactic but it's only her passion for the wines getting the better of her. And they are very good indeed – not cheap, but of excellent quality because of the low yields. There's real commitment here, both to the wines and to the region as a whole.

The wine road now leads past **Ribeauvillé**. Here we enter honeypot territory, the villages most popular with tourists. Ribeauvillé centre is pedestrianized and worth a stroll, perhaps stopping at the restaurant Zum Pfifferhüs, which offers regional specialities in a building classed as a historic monument. Then, if you take the right turn at the traffic lights just after the village centre, you'll come to a pottery on the left after about 200m. Alsace is famous for its traditional ceramics – distinctive floral patterns on a blue or brown background – and there's an excellent selection here, reasonably priced, including *kugelhopf* moulds and casseroles for *baeckeoffe*. There's also a range of wine coolers and jugs, some festooned with bunches of grapes.

Next, turn left off the wine route for **Zellenberg**. Here I saw my first Alsace storks. Actually this is where most of France saw its first Alsace storks – the nesting, birth and development of a stork family was filmed from Zellenberg's church tower by French television last year, with regular updates. I gather it did wonders for local tourism.

JEAN BECKER and **GASTON BECK,** based in the village, are the same firm, now run by the 13th generation. Martine Becker-Beck is Sales Manager, and if she's not on one of her sales trips she'll be on duty in the company's large, rustic tasting-room. Martine is extremely knowledgeable about local wines and history. The estate offers a range from generic to Grand Cru, all bearing the stamp of good winemaking. Even the Sylvaner is lively, clean and refreshing. For grapes grown in their Grand Cru vineyard, Froehn, which are not allowed to be designated as Grand Cru wine, they've put the letter 'F' on the label. Martine is equally at home taking you through the basic differences in taste between the Alsace grape varieties as she is in dissecting finer points of oenology with experts. There's a good range of *eaux-de-vie*, from wild raspberry to holly, of all things, and a worthwhile cellar tour. She may even stay open at lunch-time.

The Schlossberg hotel offers a friendly welcome and a cosy dining-room with honest regional cooking, popular with locals. The owners often exchange customers with Maximilien, the village's Michelin-starred restaurant, so you can eat one night at each. They're very informative about local history and can offer a brochure (in French only) describing a 'historical circuit' of the village. Pricey rooms, in rustic style with sombre, dark wood, are housed separately across the road. Some have terraces with views across to Riquewihr.

The medieval town of **Riquewihr** is a vital stop on any wine tour. It has an unrivalled collection of 16th, 17th and 18th century half-timbered and stone buildings. The surrounding vineyards are some of the region's finest, and one of the reasons for the early settlement and importance of the town. Its old ramparts and defences remain in evidence and many old-established wine firms still do business here.

A good example is **DOPFF & IRION**, and you can visit the estate in two ways. If you turn up on spec you are invited into a long, decorative tasting-cellar. Here you can stand at the bar and sample the range. If you make an appointment, however, you can make a half-hour tour of the cellars. This takes you through the fermentation and maturation areas, avoiding the more 'industrial' sights of wine production such as storage pallets, and includes a room with old winepresses apparently supporting the ceiling. The room also contains large wooden barrels, the oldest dating back to 1783, which were last put into service in 1982. In that year the harvest was one and a half times the usual size and every available container was commandeered, including railway tankers and even swimming-pools.

The wines at Dopff & Irion are firm and dry, and very well made. Generics start at FF22 for an Edelzwicker and prices rise steeply thereafter. The Crémant, at FF42–49, is impressively rich. They'll also sell you *eaux-de-vie* and plenty of gifts packs.

From Riquewihr or Zellenberg you can follow the Grand Cru vineyard footpath. It's about 15km long, and leads you through the main vineyards with some stunning views. The path is waymarked and you can pick up a map at one of the local tourist information offices or at properties nearby. The map also shows ways of shortening the route.

From Riquewihr the wine road itself passes through Bennwihr and Mittelwihr. These villages were heavily bombed in the closing stages of the Second World War and have little charm, so I suggest taking the narrow vineyard road from Riquewihr direct to **Kientzheim**, which is very picturesque. (It's easier to find when coming from the other direction, so you may prefer to incorporate it in your return journey. To do this, drive past the fountain in Kientzheim and take the road straight ahead of you heading out into the vines.)

Kientzheim has a wine museum in the château which houses the Confrérie de St-Etienne, the local brotherhood (sisters occasionally allowed) devoted to the promotion of Alsace wine. A good place to stay is at the Abbaye d'Alspach, attractively converted in rustic Alsace style, with a tower and open wooden walkways. There's no restaurant but plenty of advice is given on where to eat locally. I think it's a better bet to stay here than in boisterously touristy Kaysersberg up the road.

The estate to visit in Kientzheim is **PAUL BLANCK & FILS**. Its tasting-cellars are full of curiosities, including a collection of caged puppets whirring around on the tops of barrels. There's a relaxed atmosphere for the tasting and explanation of the wines – which are extremely good. If you're keen to learn, allow one and a half to two hours. Marcel Blanck, the winemaker, is big and generous; so are his wines.

There's another informative wine trail from Kientzheim, taking you through the Grand Cru vineyards. Local properties can provide a map. Look out for a slightly surreal, three-part sculpture in memory of Josef Schwartz, guiding force behind the introduction of the Grands Crus.

Cooperatives are particularly significant in Alsace, where many growers produce on too small a scale to vinify their grapes themselves. Co-ops supply a large percentage of the wines we drink in the UK and there's a tendency to think they produce quantity rather than quality. Sometimes I believe that's true, and whereas co-ops are easy places to buy wine, particularly for the novice, they won't give you the personal contact a small-scale grower can. The **CAVE VINICOLE DE KIENTZHEIM/KAYSERSBERG**, however, has an outstanding reputation for quality. Formed in 1955 with 150 members, it was the first in the region to install electronic quality-selection and -monitoring equipment, in 1976. Now it produces an average of 1.7M bottles a year.

Dealing with huge volumes of grapes arriving at the cellar each day throughout the harvest used to leave farmers queuing up with trailer-loads of grapes until well past midnight, waiting for them to be graded and weighed – bad for the farmer who had to be up and out again at the crack of dawn, bad for the grapes which suffered a deterioration in quality when exposed for hours to the air. Now everything is computerized and the grapes are vinified separately according to their variety, quality and place of origin (and farmers are paid strictly in accordance with the quality of what they produce). The separate wines are tracked by computer right through the cellar.

A free multilingual tour is offered each week during the summer and it's well worth attending just to see the complexity of an operation on this scale. There's excellent Crémant (kept on its lees twice as long as the law demands) and good varietal character in all the wines, which can be tried in two tasting-rooms: a modern one, in the main building at Kientzheim (signposted off the Kientzheim bypass), and another, in rustic style, on the main street in Kaysersberg.

Ammerschwihr was 'compulsorily redeveloped' in the closing days of the Second World War and most of its ancient centre was destroyed. There's a small hotel, A l'Arbre Vert, with good regional cooking and topiary in the dining-room. The village is also worth stopping at for the small family firm of **Sick-Dreyer** (on the D11I between Ammerschwihr and Kientzheim).

One of the first winegrowers I ever visited, because I'd enjoyed her wines from a UK merchant, Mme Dreyer offered a warm, friendly welcome despite my breaking most of the rules by turning up unannounced in the middle of the harvest (it was probably lunch-time, too). These are wines of great finesse, particularly those from her beloved Kaefferkopf vineyard (plenty of politics here, for those who are interested, on why this isn't a Grand Cru site).

Mme Dreyer takes the opposite view to those producers who like to keep separate the wines made from different sites: she believes that mixing the grapes grown on all the various soils within the vineyard produces a richer, more complex and harmonious wine. Faced with the evidence in the glass, how can I disagree? The firm no longer exports to the UK, after an unhappy business experience. Redress the balance by buying direct.

The wines of the **ZIND-HUMBRECHT** estate, on the other hand, are widely available in the UK and regularly walk off with batches of prizes in international wine competitions. Father and son Leonard and Olivier Humbrecht make wine together. Olivier has studied winemaking all over the world and is one of the first non-British Masters of Wine.

They have recently built a new winery among the vines on the D11 just outside **Turckheim** and it's an architect's dream – a brilliant, striking, modern design. Indeed, while I was there about a hundred architects were being shown round, a little the worse for wear after lunch and looking enviously at us while we were tasting.

English language tastings are conducted by Olivier's Scottish wife Margaret (they met on a London bus). The domaine isn't prepared for impromptu visits and doesn't encourage tourists. It's vital to make an appointment. You'll be rewarded by a tasting of four or five excellent wines, depending on what is currently open, and a careful explanation of the range, tailored to your level of interest. Margaret says she would rather devote an hour to explaining the wines in detail in this way than cater for casual visitors.

Here is a graphic example of just how much you can save by buying direct from the vineyard: a '91 Sylvaner is on sale in Wine Rack for perhaps £6.50 but you can buy the '92 from the domaine for just FF30. At the other end of the range, the '90 Clos Windsbühl Gewurztraminer costs about £16 in Wine Rack and the '92 is FF80 at source. If you've tasted the '90, you might be forgiven for thinking that the estate is keen to produce very powerful, intense, overblown Gewurztraminer. The '92 is much more restrained, however, and closer to the domaine's preferred style.

Fans of American wine guru Robert Parker may recall that he awarded the '89 Clos Windsbühl Gewurztraminer his ultimate accolade, 100/100. This threw the estate into confusion. The

Humbrechts had only recently acquired the Windsbühl vineyard and 1989 was the first year they made wine from it. By the time Parker's rating was published all the wine had been shipped, and the first they knew of their success was when irate customers began to phone, demanding to know why they hadn't been allocated more of it. Robert Parker considers the Humbrechts to be among the great winemakers of the world, and I couldn't disagree.

From Turckheim to **Wintzenheim** is a short, if dull, hop. Wintzenheim has little of the charm of most Alsace villages but in the main street, well hidden, is the estate of **JOS MEYER**. A charming, small tasting-room off a cobbled courtyard offers high-quality, elegant wines, on the dear side. There's very good Pinot Blanc, and Riesling Les Pierrets '88 at FF62.

Colmar is next on the agenda. The prospect of driving into Colmar deters all but the brave but it's worth it for the atmosphere and architecture of the pedestrianized old town. The faint-hearted could consider parking on the outskirts and walking in (the town is fairly compact) but if you feel like staying here try the Hôtel St-Martin, which comes complete with a 16th century spiral staircase and Renaissance turret. The hotel is well signposted – you're directed to park in a square outside the police station, a couple of minutes' walk away. Rooms are comfortable and spread over a wide price range.

The St-Martin doesn't have a restaurant, so head for one of Colmar's many *winstubs*. My favourite is S'Parisser Stewwele, five minutes from the hotel. It heaves with local couples and parties who come for terrific food such as *schieffala* (shoulder of pork) and wonderful *crème brûlée*. Alsace wines are available in jug or bottle; the staff are jovial and efficient. Do book. For more refinement there's Maison des Têtes, in a beautiful 17th century building with about a hundred carved heads decorating the front. Good picnic *charcuterie* can be found at Glasser on Rue des Boulangers and at La Ferme on Rue des Têtes; there's excellent bread at Léonard Helmstetter on Rue des Serruriers.

Walk through the old town and look out for the painted façade of Maison Pfister, the Tanners' Quarter and Little Venice down by the river. Then there is also the famous Isenheim altarpiece in the Unterlinden Museum... best to visit the tourist information office, or ask the hotel to show you where everything is, if you have time to spend half a day here.

The next port of call is **Eguisheim**, one of my favourite villages for the perfectly preserved ramparts which encircle it. (You can walk right round, following signs marked *circuit de visite*.) It gets very busy in season, so I would go early in summer. As you stroll through the streets, open courtyards reveal modern winemaking equipment squeezed in under half-timbered buildings. This is still a working village. In the central square is a good restaurant, Le Caveau d'Eguisheim, offering traditional dishes in very large helpings.

Husseren-les-Châteaux, above Eguisheim, is the starting-point for the diversion along the signposted Route des 5 Châteaux. It's also the home of **Kuentz-Bas**, offering a small, rustic tasting-room and a selection of two ranges. Cuvée Tradition is made from bought-in grapes and designed to be drunk young; Réserve Personnelle is from Kuentz-Bas' own vineyards and has more ageing potential.

The wine route now meanders through some rather uninteresting villages and eventually forces you onto the main dual carriageway (the N83). Since you've got to use this road in the end, I suggest you join it sooner rather than later, bypassing Pfaffenheim and Rouffach and heading direct for **Westhalten**.

Just as you turn off the dual carriageway for Westhalten you come to the estate of **René Muré**, which is well worth a visit. It has a series of small, elegantly-furnished tasting-rooms and the main one has a glorious view overlooking the estate's principal vineyard, the Clos St-Landelin, facing up the valley to Westhalten. A tour of the cellars will show you a 13th century winepress, the oldest in Alsace, and a family tree dating back to 1620. This is a very easy place to visit; you don't need an appointment, there are several English-speaking staff dedicated to welcoming visitors and they are just as happy giving a beginner's guide to the wines as comparing particular vintages and soils. These are excellent wines, with a recognizable, soft, fruity house style.

From here it's a short drive up to Westhalten to my favourite Alsace hotel, the Auberge Cheval Blanc, which has a dozen rooms in an annexe built five years ago which looks out over the valley. I find a great sense of contentment gazing at this view in the evening. The restaurant is Alsacien in furnishing and food – the FF150 menu is good value and the *foie gras* and *rognons de veau* (calves' kidneys) are excellent. The family makes its own wine – honest generic *appellations* – which you can try out over dinner and maybe buy a case of. A generous buffet breakfast is provided, if you still have room, and then perhaps you could try the lovely vineyard walk (the hotel has maps). They don't get many British visitors here, and those that arrive receive a very warm welcome.

And for me, this is where the road ends. The wine route carries on for 30km yet, but the scenery becomes less attractive and the towns not so interesting. The character becomes less Alsacien, more Vosgesien, and by the time you get to Thann you're surrounded by pine forests, logging yards and sawmills – it almost looks as though you've strayed into Twin Peaks. You can either cut through the Vosges mountains and head up to the motorway via Nancy (which is really doing things the hard way) or, better, turn around and visit the places you missed on the way down – perhaps picking up the Route of the Fried Pike-Perch.

Listings

When telephoning France from the UK, the number must be preceded by the digits 010 33. Producers are listed in wine route order, and hotels/restaurants by town or village according to the route. Accommodation prices are per room, meal prices are per head.

Producers

Domaine Klipfel
1 rue Rotland, 67140 Barr
Tel 88 08 94 85, Fax 88 08 53 18
Open Mon–Sun 10–12, 14–18
Credit cards accepted
Some English

Domaine André & Rémy Gresser
2 rue de l'Ecole, 67140 Andlau
Tel 88 08 95 88, Fax 88 08 55 99
Open Mon–Sun 10–12, 14–19
Good English

Domaine Ostertag
87 rue Finkwiller, 67680 Epfig
Tel 88 85 51 44
Visits by appointment (for tutored tasting on Sat, in French only, phone 2 weeks in advance)
Good English

Klein aux Vieux Remparts
Route du Haut-Koenigsbourg, 68590 St-Hippolyte
Tel 89 73 00 41, Fax 89 73 04 94
Visits by appointment
Good English

Rolly Gassmann
1 rue de l'Eglise, 68590 Rorschwihr
Tel 89 73 63 28, Fax 89 73 33 06
Open Mon–Sat 8–12, 13–19
No English

Marcel Deiss
15 route du Vin, 68750 Bergheim
Tel 89 73 63 37, Fax 89 73 32 67
Open Mon–Sat 10–12, 14–18
Credit cards accepted
Some English

Jean Becker/Gaston Beck
2–4 route d'Ostheim, 68340 Zellenberg
Tel 89 47 90 16, Fax 89 47 99 57
Open Mon–Sun 8–12, 14–18; possibly also open lunch-time
Good English

Dopff & Irion
Au Château de Riquewihr,
68340 Riquewihr
Tel 89 47 92 51, Fax 89 47 92 51
Tasting-cellar open Mon–Sun 8–18 incl lunch-time; tour of cellars by appointment
Credit cards accepted
Some English

Paul Blanck & Fils
32 Grand-Rue, 68240 Kientzheim
Tel 89 78 23 56, Fax 89 47 16 45
Open Mon–Sat 9–12, 14–17.30
Some English

Cave Vinicole de Kientzheim/
  Kaysersberg
68240 Kientzheim (& 68240 Kaysersberg)
Tel 89 47 13 19, Fax 89 47 34 38

Open at Kientzheim Mon–Thurs 8–12,
14–18, Fri 8–12, 14–17,
Sat & Sun 10–12, 14–18; cellar tour July
& Aug Wed at 15.00, approx 1 hour,
no booking necessary, multilingual
Open at Kaysersberg Easter–11 Nov
Mon–Sun

Sick-Dreyer
17 route de Kientzheim,
68770 Ammerschwihr
Tel 89 47 11 31, Fax 89 47 32 60
Visits by appointment
No English

Zind-Humbrecht
4 route du Colmar, 68230 Turckheim
Tel 89 27 02 05, Fax 89 27 22 58
Visits by appointment Mon–Fri pm
English: 'like a native'

Jos Meyer
76 rue Clémenceau,
68920 Wintzenheim
Tel 89 27 01 57, Fax 89 27 03 98
Open Mon–Fri 10–12, 14–17
Good English

An additional visit: Robert Schoffit
27 rue des Aubépines, 68000 Colmar
Tel 89 24 41 14, Fax 89 41 40 52
Open Mon–Sat 8.30–12, 14–17;
visits by appointment Sun
Some English
(A rising star using traditional methods.)

Kuentz-Bas
14 route du Vin,
68420 Husseren-les-Châteaux
Tel 89 49 30 24, Fax 89 49 23 39
Open autumn & winter Mon–Fri 9–12,
13.30–18, Sat 10–12; spring & summer
also open pm
Good English

René Muré
Clos St-Landelin,
Route du Vin, 68250 Rouffach
Tel 89 49 62 19, Fax 89 49 74 85
Open Mon–Fri 8–18, Sat 8–12, 14–18,
Sun 10–12, 14–18; closed Nov–spring
on Sun (except last 2 Sun before
Christmas)
Good English

Hotels and Restaurants
H Hotel   *R* Restaurant

Hinsingen
R La Grange du Paysan
8 rue Principale
Tel 88 00 91 83
FF61–245

La Petite-Pierre
HR Auberge d'Imsthal
Route Forestière d'Imsthal,
67290 La Petite-Pierre
Tel 88 70 45 21, Fax 88 70 40 26
Rooms FF220–600, Meals FF80–230

HR Aux Trois Roses
67290 La Petite-Pierre
Tel 88 89 89 00, Fax 88 70 41 28
Rooms FF315–530, Meals FF97–245

Strasbourg
HR Sofitel
Place St-Pierre-le-Jeune,
67000 Strasbourg
Tel 88 32 99 30, Fax 88 32 60 67
Rooms FF650–800, Meals FF130–210

H Hôtel des Rohan
17 rue Maroquin,
67000 Strasbourg
Tel 88 32 85 11, Fax 88 75 65 37
FF350–595

R Maison Kammerzell
16 place Cathédrale
Tel 88 32 42 14
FF190–260
(There are also a few rooms upstairs, in
Hôtel Baumann, for FF420–630.)

R S'Burjerstuewel (Chez Yvonne)
10 rue Sanglier
Tel 88 32 84 15
FF170–210

R Zum Strissel
5 place Grande Boucherie
Tel 88 32 14 73
FF56–130

Andlau
H Zinck-Hôtel
13 rue de la Marne, 67140 Andlau
Tel 88 08 27 30, Fax 88 08 42 50
FF250–500

R Au Boeuf Rouge
6 rue Dr-Stoltz
Tel 88 08 96 26
FF165–245

R Le Relais de la Poste
1 rue des Forgerons
Tel 88 08 95 91
FF65–135

Itterswiller
HR Hôtel Arnold
98 route du Vin, 67140 Itterswiller
Tel 88 85 50 58, Fax 88 85 55 54
Rooms FF440–695, Meals FF150–385

St-Hippolyte
HR Aux Ducs de Lorraine
16 route du Vin, 68590 St-Hippolyte
Tel 89 73 00 09, Fax 89 73 05 46
Rooms FF450–600, Meals FF100–300
(member of Relais du Silence)

Sélestat
HR Hostellerie de l'Abbaye
  La Pommeraie
8 avenue Foch, 67600 Sélestat
Tel 88 92 07 84, Fax 88 92 08 71
Rooms FF690–1,500, Meals FF230–450

Thannenkirch
HR Auberge La Meunière
30 rue Ste-Anne, 68590 Thannenkirch
Tel 89 73 10 47, Fax 89 73 12 31
Rooms FF250–310, Meals FF95–180

Bergheim
R Wistub du Sommelier
51 Grand'Rue
Tel 89 73 69 99, Fax 89 73 36 58
FF150–230

Ribeauvillé
R Zum Pfifferhüs
14 Grand'Rue
Tel 89 73 62 28
FF140–190

Zellenberg
HR Le Schlossberg
59A rue de la Fontaine,
68340 Zellenberg
Tel 89 47 93 85, Fax 89 47 82 40
Rooms FF300–550, Meals FF85–230

R Maximilien
19A route d'Ostheim
Tel 89 47 99 69
FF185–360

Kientzheim
H L'Abbaye d'Alspach
2–4 rue Foch, 68240 Kientzheim
Tel 89 47 16 00, Fax 89 78 29 73
FF220–400

Ammerschwihr
HR A l'Arbre Vert
4 rue des Cigognes,
68770 Ammerschwihr
Tel 89 47 12 23, Fax 89 78 27 21
Rooms FF100–350, Meals FF70–210

Colmar
H Hôtel St-Martin
38 Grand'Rue, 68000 Colmar
Tel 89 24 11 51, Fax 89 23 47 78
FF300–620

R S'Parisser Stewwele
4 place Jeanne-d'Arc
Tel 89 41 42 33, Fax 89 41 37 99
FF120–320

R Maison des Têtes
19 rue Têtes
Tel 89 24 43 43
FF130–300

Eguisheim
R Le Caveau d'Eguisheim
3 place Château
Tel 89 41 08 89, Fax 89 23 79 99
FF130–335

Westhalten
HR Auberge Cheval Blanc
29 rue Rouffach, 68250 Westhalten
Tel 89 47 01 16, Fax 89 47 64 40
Rooms FF300–450, Meals FF150–400

The Golden Triangle

Three separate winemaking areas cluster together in northern France, and by accidents of geography they each produce different styles of wine. This means that the intrepid explorer can find wines from Champagne, Burgundy and the Loire Valley without the tedium of travelling long distances: you can visit all three regions in one long weekend. (The map on page 8 shows how these winemaking areas are grouped.) The Aube offers the best value and the best scenery in Champagne; Chablis makes fashionable white burgundy, while its satellite villages offer cheaper whites, surprisingly attractive reds and good-quality sparklers; Sancerre's hilltop setting is spectacular and its crisp white wines are prized throughout the world.

PLANNING THE ROUTE

This so-called triangle is more of a Golden Straight Line. It takes about four hours to reach the Aube on the A26 from Calais, and not much longer from Ostend. The new Paris–Troyes motorway makes travel via Paris an option and Le Havre an attractive second bet to Calais. For Chablis, you can either travel via Paris and the A6 to Auxerre, or take the A26 as far as Troyes and then D roads via Chaource and Tonnerre. Sancerre has no motorway link at present (although the N7 is to be upgraded to a toll-free motorway). Take the A6 from Paris and turn off onto the N5.

The Aube

This is Champagne's Cinderella, maligned and ignored. So far south of the focus of commerce in Reims, its voice went unheeded until very recently, and the grand houses in Reims looked down their noses at it. No Grandes Marques are found here, and much has been made of the supposed inferior quality of Aube champagne.

The big names like to imply that all the grapes they use to make champagne come from only the very best villages on the Montagne de Reims and the Côte des Blancs, yet these sites account for as little as 15–20% of the total production. They simply won't admit to the fact that nearly all of them buy grapes from the Aube. The region produces the equivalent of about 50M bottles a year, but only about 10M bottles are shipped from the area, in other words are identifiably Aube wines. The rest, 40M bottles' worth, finds its way north, adding its weight to wines made by houses based in Reims and Epernay.

Times are changing, however. As one Aube grower said: 'The big houses are no longer saying the wines are no good in the Aube, because everyone knows they buy here'. The predominant grape in this area is Pinot Noir, which lends structure and depth, and is needed by the big Reims names to enhance their blends.

Nowadays several names are emerging from the Aube to challenge the supposed superiority of Reims and Epernay winemakers. They are gaining a reputation through good results in blind tastings; and as the trend in champagne flavour moves away from light, lemony tastes to heavier, more aromatic blends, Aube wines stand to gain a great deal of ground.

EXPLORING THE AUBE

In an effort to distance themselves from the old days of bad reputations and bulk winemaking, Aube producers have begun to refer to this area as the 'Côte des Bar', taking their cue from the more northerly – and prestigious – Côte des Blancs. It sounds like a good idea to me (well, it worked for Windscale).

The winemaking area is indeed bounded by Bars: Bar-sur-Aube in the east and Bar-sur-Seine in the west. Both these are attractive towns, well worth visiting in their own right; but the best starting-point is **Troyes**, the regional capital and as yet undiscovered by British tourists.

Troyes had the good fortune to be among the first 15 towns and cities singled out for restoration and conservation by the French government in the 1960s. As a result its old town is remarkably intact, with a mixture of half-timbered buildings leaning at eccentric angles and Renaissance architecture which replaced the razed wooden buildings after a fire in the 16th century. Local stonemasons adopted the cabbage as a carving motif, and in the cathedral there's even a chomping snail carved into one. Troyes was famous for medieval fairs and markets, and is where Troy weights come from (but not Helen, or the wooden horse).

The city is also famous for its *andouillettes*, sausages of pig intestine stuffed with tripe. (Yum.) Apparently in 1560 the king's army attempted to capture Troyes from the Governor of Champagne. Unfortunately, the king's soldiers dawdled on the outskirts of the city searching for *andouillettes*, whereupon they were surprised and repulsed.

It's the kind of place where you can spend an afternoon wandering around the old town, or days exploring all the museums and churches. The atmosphere is relatively unspoilt by tourism because the city is not on the tour operators' traditional map; no doubt that will slowly change once people begin to take advantage of the new motorway connections, so now is a good time to go.

Right in the centre (but well signposted) is the Hôtel la Poste: smart rooms and glitzy bathrooms, fairly priced, and good breakfasts, less fairly priced. It boasts no fewer than three restaurants, from a pizzeria to *haute cuisine*. The middle restaurant, Bistro de la Mer, decked out like a yacht, offers impressively fresh seafood. Rather easier to find, near the tourist office and station, is the Royal Hôtel.

Leave Troyes on the N71 in the direction of Dijon, and the first port of call is **Bar-sur-Seine**, capital of Auboise Champagne. The town is cut in two by the River Seine and has more attractive half-timbered buildings and churches. Just south of Bar, off the N71 at **Merrey-sur-Arce**, is the first visit, the **UNION AUBOISE**, with its brand, Veuve A Devaux.

The Union Auboise is a super-co-op, a grouping formed 25 years ago by 12 cooperatives to give themselves sufficient financial clout to afford a decent cellar-master and a marketing budget. It's big: 750 producers, 1,200ha of vines, about 3M bottles a year. Quality picked up slowly but the co-op is now winning prizes, especially with its rosé champagnes (a strength in the area as a whole, and based on the use of red wines made from Pinot Noir).

Seven years ago the Union bought itself a slice of history when it acquired the old Epernay champagne house of Devaux, which was one of the first Grandes Marques but had fallen into decline. Buying Devaux enabled the Union to announce that its house was formed in 1846 rather than 1967. (It's common nowadays for cooperatives to use brands rather than to trade under the co-op name: Le Brun de Neuville (qv) in the Sézannais is another example.)

The cooperative's labelling and packaging is glamorous and the champagnes are of very good quality, although dearer than those from small-scale growers. A shiny new visitors' centre, where you can taste and buy and see various exhibitions, is to open shortly but there's no opportunity for casual visitors to tour the cellars. For one thing, being situated on the banks of the River Seine means that the water-table is just one metre down, making underground cellaring impossible – so there are no romantic caves to visit. Romance also flies out of the window when you see the co-op's huge, automated bottling-lines in operation.

If you're interested in watching 4,000 bottles an hour being processed, however, just make an appointment; they will be delighted to show you round and explain the different stages. I love watching mechanical processes, and here there's a fully-automated packing line, from folding the cardboard boxes onwards. The maturation cellars are temperature controlled and even have sensors inside a bottle in each batch; electronic controls display read-outs and bring temperatures into line at the flick of a switch.

Go through Merrey and pick up the D4 to Ville-sur-Arce. Two things immediately become apparent: the scenery here is much more attractive than in the northern part of Champagne, and the sign-posting is much worse. Although there is an official *route du vin* down here, the lack of attention the Aube receives means that it hasn't been given the same investment as the route around Epernay. (Indeed, the big glossy map of the Champagne wine route handed out by tourist offices in Reims and its wine committee ignores the Aube altogether – very supportive.) I do believe this will change. Meanwhile, try this route or just follow your instinct and meander around the very pretty countryside.

From Ville, the route enters Landreville and Chacenay before settling down on the D4 again. After Bligny, turn right on the D44 to **Urville**, where **ANDRÉ DRAPPIER** is based. You're welcomed in a large, comfortable tasting-room; sit out on the terrace in summer or enjoy their log fire in winter. Access to the cellars, parts of which were built in 1152 by Cistercian monks, is via a spiral staircase at one end of the tasting-room. There you can hear an explanation of the firm's winemaking processes given in immaculate English.

One of Drappier's specialities is the production of large bottles. Most houses making magnums, jeroboams or what have you will make the champagne in ordinary-sized bottles and simply pour the finished product into bigger ones. It's much harder to complete the second fermentation in larger bottles, as Drappier does. For one thing, the bottles are not machine-made so they are much more likely to explode under the pressure of second fermentation. Michel Drappier says he can lose up to 40% of his bottles this way but believes it's worth it because of the improved quality of the champagne.

This is a family firm, with some of the best vineyards in Urville under its control. The wines are full-flavoured and rich. Michel recognizes the disadvantages of being hidden away in an unknown village at the unfashionable end of Champagne: 'If you want to be at the top, being in Reims is better'. Accordingly, the Drappiers own maturation cellars in the city, which entitles them to put the magic word 'Reims' on the label, but it's clear they're proud of the individual identity of their Côte des Bar wines.

They offer a range starting at FF75, rising to the splendid prestige *cuvée*, Grande Cendrée. If they still have the '85, for FF116, treat yourself (and try the later vintages, too). The bottle is gorgeous: a long-necked, low-slung shape based on an old bottle they found lying in the cellar and copyrighted. The champagne is full of the richness that comes from old vines and from the *tête de cuvée* (the best of the first pressing).

If you're looking for other gift ideas they'll sell you a champagne bottle filled with liqueur chocolates, or a chic black wine cooler. I was impressed by Drappier, both for the quality of the champagne and for the quality of the visit. I believe you'll find a warm welcome here, and every reason to come out afterwards convinced that the Aube has been maligned for far too long.

From Urville it's a short hop to **Bar-sur-Aube**. (D170–D101–D201 and back on the D4.) The journey is shorter than it sounds and worth the complicated route for the scenic pleasures. There's also a splendid view of the Aube Valley from the top of a very steep track off to the right of the D4 at Ste-Germaine.

Bar-sur-Aube is the sort of place I always think of as 'undiscovered France': gently-paced, with few tourists, the air heavy with wood-smoke, and full of unannounced architectural pleasures, such as the wooden gallery on the side of the ancient church, which once housed a market.

Stay at the Relais des Gouverneurs on the town's main street. It's a member of Logis de France and exactly what a Logis should be, with a warm welcome, friendly and efficient staff, and comfortable rooms of the creaky-traditional, floral-wallpaper-on-every-surface variety. Breakfast is exemplary. Dinner, too, is excellent, and great value; the FF88 menu is a snip, and everything is made in-house, from the bread to the sorbets.

A detour if Général de Gaulle interests you; he's buried in the churchyard at Colombey-les-deux-Eglises, near Bar on the N19. A huge cross of Lorraine has been erected in his memory on a nearby hillside. It can be seen for miles.

Leave Bar on the D396 and turn off onto the D70 for Baroville. Follow this road to **Essoyes**, across attractive open countryside. This area isn't particularly strong on restaurants but offers plenty of pretty, unofficial picnic sites. Essoyes, apart from being a pleasant village worth a stroll, is home to a wine museum open during the summer. A clutch of Renoirs is buried here. From Essoyes head back up into the hills towards Gyé-sur-Seine (along the D67 and D103), and from there join the D70 into Les Riceys.

Les Riceys is plural because there are three of them (I found this out the hard way). If you keep turning left when you come into the cluster of villages on the D70 you'll end up on the D17 which climbs steeply; there's a picnic site halfway up the hill on the right, which offers you a commanding view.

Heading back down the D17 and into the villages again, Ricey-Haut is the first Ricey you come to, with Ricey-Bas beyond. Once you've strolled through the winding streets and inspected the three churches, head for Ricey-Bas on the D452 Bar-sur-Seine road. Turn left at the far side of the village, signposted D142 Avirey, and **DOMAINE MICHEL NOIROT** is on the right. As you drive through the arch you're met by rose-beds and a slightly decaying château; the Noirots bought the house a decade ago because they fell in love with it, but ever since have sunk their money into the winemaking rather than their home.

I thought Mme Noirot looked a little like Simone Signoret; she's very friendly and laid-back, smokes like a chimney, and is always accompanied by her neighbour's dog. She rescued this dog when it fell behind a bank of maturing champagne bottles and lay trapped for a fortnight; now it follows her everywhere in gratitude, much to the neighbour's annoyance.

To visit here is to discover a champagne house in formation. Until 1993 M Noirot sold part of his harvest by the kilogram, for cash flow, while vinifying the rest himself and slowly building up a good reputation. But in 1993 he cast himself free and vinified all the crop himself. He's used no chemical fertilizers in the vineyard for the past seven years, ploughing and manuring instead.

Things being at an early stage here, you taste standing around a table in one corner of the cellar. They plan something more comfortable, but I think being in the middle of a working cellar is more fun. Unusually for the Aube, where Chardonnay accounts for less than 10% of plantings, the Noirots make a *blanc de blancs* from white grapes (in other words, from Chardonnay only). It's pale and delicate, unlike the more robust character of other Aube wines. Their standard non-vintage is light, too, fresh and lively with lots of fruit. If the vintage 1985, a full, rich champagne, is still available it's well worth trying. A range of elegant, light-bodied wines from a full-bodied couple, unpretentious and friendly.

Les Riceys just about completes the circuit. From here you can head back to Troyes and home or visit Chaource, 22km west of Les Riceys, home of one of my favourite cheeses and also the church of St-John the Baptist, with remarkable artworks. Or, again, you can head directly for Chablis, next stop on the golden-straight-line tour, via the pretty D452 to Tonnerre.

Chablis

Chablis is Burgundy's northern outpost, an isolated winemaking area just about as far north as you can get grapes to ripen. It's famous for its Chardonnay whites, which differ from their southern Burgundy counterparts in their higher acidity (the result of a northern climate) and their minerally taste (the product of a chalky-clay soil).

Naturally, this being France, there's a hierarchy of wines. Generic Chablis is what there's most of – it accounts for 64% of production. Below that there's Petit Chablis, accounting for less than a quarter. This is a relatively new name (cashing in on Chablis' fame, according to some), the vines are planted on poorer slopes and the wines are all too often lacking in decent taste and varietal character. Above generic Chablis there are Premiers Crus (accounting for 11%) and Grands Crus (2%). These are the best the region has to offer and are priced accordingly. Petit Chablis is best drunk young, if at all, Chablis within three years of the vintage, the Premiers Crus at five to eight years and the Grands Crus from eight years.

Being so far north, the angle of the vineyard towards the sun is vital in order to gain every available second of sunshine. The top vineyards occupy the best positions, but these sites also leave the vines highly vulnerable to frost. If you're here in late spring you will see all kinds of measures being taken to protect the delicate buds, from the positioning of braziers to spraying the vines with water (which forms a protective frozen cover over the buds).

The winemakers are deeply divided over what Chablis should taste like – a fairly basic question, you might think. One camp ferments and ages the wine in wood, and believes the extra structure this lends the wine helps it to age well; the other insists that the flavours of wood can overwhelm the natural delicate mineral flavour of proper Chablis, and that the region shouldn't try to imitate its cousins further south. Which is better? I leave that for you to decide. For my part, I find the arguments of each grower, at the moment I hear them in the cellar with a glass in my hand, overwhelmingly persuasive. Then, in the next cellar where I hear the opposing view, I'm equally convinced.

EXPLORING CHABLIS

I've identified three elements to a tour of the area. The first part of the visit is centred on Chablis itself and within walking distance of the hotels – handy for tasting without having to drive. The second part covers 'Chablis satellites' around the village, by car, and the third takes you further afield, visiting the vineyards near the River Yonne.

Chablis the village is surprisingly dull and modern. Not its fault – it was bombed nearly to bits in June 1940 and the rebuild has all the excitement and verve you'd expect of 1950s architecture. Stay either at L'Etoile or Hostellerie des Clos, both of which are in the centre. L'Etoile is cheap, and certain rooms (notably number seven) have been refurbished with some style. At its most basic you can get a very floral room without a bath for just FF140. The cooking is so-so. At the Hostellerie des Clos the food is Michelin-starred (but service is very slow when it's busy) and rooms are expensive and fancy. Restaurant Le Vieux Moulin, close to L'Etoile, has a mill-race rushing beneath and offers good local ham dishes.

Call in at the Maison du Vin for maps and advice; it's in the same building as the tourist information office and well signposted. Then begin your visits to producers at the local cooperative, **LA CHABLISIENNE**. This is a powerful local player, controlling one-third of the Chablis crop. The cellar tasting-room has a long counter with a background of barrels, some of which are glass-fronted and lit so you can see the maturing wine within. It's an easy, relaxed place to taste. The Petit Chablis and especially the Chablis are full of

N

CHABLIS

♥ Wine producer
H Hotel
R Restaurant
See Listings
pages 193–5
for further details

flavour and at fair prices for the area. Basic reds are also available. They'll show you the cellars if time permits, but you may prefer to wait for a cellar visit until you arrive at **JEAN-PAUL DROIN**.

While La Chablisienne, with its enormous production, has one foot in both oak and stainless steel camps, M Droin is firmly on the side of oak. This is a husband-and-wife operation and visits are strictly by appointment – from the outside the elegant villa doesn't look like a winemaker's premises at all. M Droin is the tenth generation to farm the estate ('the eleventh is at school'), which now produces five Grands Crus and seven Premiers Crus. His cellars are proper, romantic, subterranean caves, dimly lit and containing row after row of barrels. Here the advanced student can have a tasting and discuss (in French) the differences between the vineyard sites and the vintages, and the case for and against oak – with the evidence in favour in the glass.

Close by is the domaine of **RENÉ & VINCENT DAUVISSAT**. This is one of the most eccentric visits I've ever had the pleasure of making. The wines are unobtrusively oaked and excellent; this is winemaking of the highest quality. The Dauvissats don't go out of their way to woo the public. You may be able to get an appointment, you may be able to taste the wines, it may all be terribly vague, but it's worth persevering for the quality of what's on offer.

Some properties based outside the village have shops within and sell to the public from these rather than from the estate. Visit them by all means, but I don't think they are as much fun as a proper cellar visit, and prices can be higher than at the vineyard. If you're pushed for time, however, LE CELLIER CHABLISIEN offers a wide selection of local wines. It's run by Bernard Guyot, ex-*sommelier* of the Hostellerie des Clos, and he gives excellent advice in very good English.

The 'Chablis satellites' tour begins with DOMAINE DES MALANDES on the Auxerre road, the D965. This is on the outskirts of the village, but in walking distance of the centre. Lyne and Bernard Marchive, a friendly, unassuming couple, are very firm adherents of the use-no-oak school and make prizewinning wines in their modern cellars.

On to **Beine**, passing a reservoir created by local winemakers to supply water for spraying vines against frost. There's an excellent lunch stop just off the main road, Le Vaulignot. Enjoy high-quality, modern cooking in its smart, yellow dining-room, then head into the village.

ALAIN GEOFFROY's estate is high up in Beine. The wines here are oaked, and I thought them excellent. The Premier Cru Beauroy, in particular, is a fine wine and FF10 cheaper than the more fashionable Fourchaume. The Geoffroys are affable hosts (Mme Geoffroy speaks English), and their tasting-room is well-lit and inviting, with table and stools.

Leave Beines on an unnumbered road to La Chapelle-Vaupelteigne, passing through the high Petit Chablis vineyards. Cross the Serein on the D131A and turn right onto the D91. This takes you past all the Grand Cru sites, on your left, and then past Chablis itself, to **Fleys**.

DOMAINE DE LA MEULIÈRE is on your right, and you go straight into an attractive tasting-room in a vaulted cellar. Charming Chantal and Claude Laroche don't speak English although their daughter, who will soon be joining the business, does. Here you'll find well-made wines at fair prices, with Chablis at FF45, and Premiers Crus at FF60.

Return to Chablis and then turn left onto the D45 to **Chichée**. Didier Picq runs the family estate of **GILBERT PICQ**, and will show you the cellar opposite the domaine before offering you a tasting. His tasting-table is cut from a huge slice of elm and the tasting bottles are stored in a fridge inside an old barrel. The family only began to bottle its own wines in 1982, since when it has built up a good reputation. Look out especially for the Chablis *vieilles vignes* at FF48, lying between generic Chablis and a Premier Cru in price and quality.

From Chichée follow signs to **Nitry**. You can either turn off to Préhy first, or continue to Nitry and a rather special restaurant. La Beursaudière is folkloric in decor, with beams, dried flowers and roaring fires, and waiting staff wear regional costume. It may sound artificial but it's carried off with style. The food emphasizes regional dishes and is well cooked and presented with flair. The day I visited, the large dining-room was brim-full of local families having an outing – the place lends itself to a sense of occasion. It's fun without feeling touristy, and worth the detour.

At **Préhy**, seek out the **DOMAINE JEAN-MARC BROCARD** (follow the road behind the church). M Brocard is creating a rapidly expanding operation and offers a wide range of unoaked wines. Some of the best value lies in his non-Chablis *appellations*, such as the 'Chardonnay from around Préhy' for FF32. Most tasting takes place in the ground-floor sales area, but do ask to see the stratified wall in his cellar tasting-room. The exposed rock layers are full of fossils, some of which are still buried in my coat pocket.

From Préhy you can either loop back to Chablis via the D2 or head off to the third circuit by the River Yonne, via Chitry and the D62. **St-Bris-le-Vineux** (lovely name) is the first stop, home to the only VDQS of the area, Sauvignon de St-Bris. Production of this wine is in decline because it doesn't fetch the prices of the local AC wines, but you'll find it at several of the producers I've listed for Chablis.

BOURGOGNES BERSAN boasts some of the most wonderful mouldy cellars I've ever visited. Originally built in the 12th century to garrison soldiers, they contain the remains of a bread oven, a chute in from the street and a stone foot press. One passage runs close to the church; they suspect secret tunnels. The wines are excellent, and excellent value: Sauvignon de St-Bris or Bourgogne Chardonnay for FF29, Bourgogne Côtes d'Auxerre (a relatively new *appellation*) for FF36. No wine is made in these cellars any more, of course; they're used for a few oak barrels (of which the current winemaker's mother doesn't approve), and for visitors. The winery is on a hill above the village, all gleaming stainless steel and modern technology.

You'll also find good winemaking at **VERRET**, on the Champs-sur-Yonne road on the outskirts of St-Bris. Bruno Verret is the youngest member of the family to join the firm, after studying in Bordeaux and working in Australia. He's full of ideas and happy to explain the local wines and regulations, and to show you round the cellars before offering a tasting that includes the only locally-made sparkling wine apart from the massive local co-op's. There are Irancy reds, too, especially from the tiny Palotte vineyard. Ask him to show you the nearby riverside picnic spot.

Now continue along the D62 to **Champs-sur-Yonne**, where you can have an excellent lunch at Les Rosiers that's very good value. Try the hefty *jarret de porc* (pork knuckle) in the pretty, blue dining-room. Thus fortified, take the D362 along the river towards **Bailly**, following signs for the **CAVES DE BAILLY**. The entrance road runs steeply up the hillside, where you can park if it looks busy, but if it isn't you have the chance to drive right into the cellars, which are cut into the surrounding rock. Deep inside you'll find a huge, subterranean tasting-cavern looking like something out of a James Bond film.

As you can immediately see, this is a big operation. It's a cooperative, but one with an excellent reputation, and the largest producer of Crémant de Bourgogne, producing one-third of all that's made. You can taste for a small sum that's refundable on purchase, and in summer guided tours are available in English. The aim is commercial, certainly, but the visit is fun nonetheless.

Stay on the pretty riverside road to Vincelottes, then turn left onto the D38 to **Irancy**. This place is a little gem, making a tiny amount of red wine that's barely known in France, never mind the UK. It's a Pinot Noir wine, just like its nobler cousins on the Côte d'Or, and although Irancy is so far north, the sheltered valley aspect gives the vines good ripening conditions, so you can expect better colour and intensity than the location might suggest. Vines fight with fruit trees and sunflowers for the best spots. The village is not particularly geared to tourism and few people speak English.

First stop is with the mayor, **LÉON BIENVENU**. He makes wines of good depth and is a passionate advocate for his *appellation*, petitioning the powers that be to drop 'Bourgogne' as a prefix to the village name, insisting that the quality of the wine should be allowed to speak for itself, and that the wine should not be made to sound generic.

I found passionate commitment too in **JEAN-PIERRE COLINOT**, and you really must visit his cellars. Here is winemaking at its simplest, with open vats set into the cellar floor; some outside in the courtyard date back to the Middle Ages. The wine bubbles away at your feet. *Pigeage*, pushing the cap of grape-skins down into the must, is done with a branch with stumpy twigs at the end. I had a go and found it hard work. He immediately promised to name the vat I'd worked on Cuvée Hilary. Hmm…

Extrovert M Colinot was named Winemaker of the Year in a French magazine a couple of years ago and he's very proud of the fact. His wines are lively, juicy and will keep, particularly those from the little Palotte site. You will be warmly welcomed here.

An overnight stop with good food that was recommended to me is close by: the Auberge Les Tilleuls at **Vincelottes**. Here you are close to the A6, if you wish to return home, but if you are carrying on down to Sancerre and Pouilly-sur-Loire there's an extremely pretty route following the canal along the D100. At Châtel-Censoir this turns into the D21. Cross the river at Coulanges, then at Clamecy follow signs for Donzy and from there the directions to Pouilly-sur-Loire. It will take about a couple of hours.

Sancerre and Pouilly-sur-Loire

We have moved grape varieties again: this is now Sauvignon Blanc territory. You'll come across some Chasselas in Pouilly (cunningly called Pouilly-sur-Loire to confuse the unwary) and some reds from Pinot Noir in Sancerre, but it's mainly Sauvignon. The two towns are close, on opposite banks of the Loire, and make an obvious touring circuit. West of Sancerre lies another cluster of wine-producing villages. First there's Menetou-Salon, then, further west, Quincy and Reuilly. These produce wine similar in style to Sancerre but cheaper, which makes seeking them out all the more worthwhile.

The Loire Valley's other very well known white wine is also produced in this region: Pouilly-Fumé. 'Fumé' means 'smoked' and some people believe the name came about because the wine has a gun-flint character. An alternative explanation is that the powdery deposits which form on the Sauvignon-Blanc grapes that make this wine look rather like smoke. Pick the romantic notion you prefer.

EXPLORING SANCERRE AND
POUILLY-SUR-LOIRE

Sancerre perches high on a hill and has an old town full of meandering streets (a little like Chinon). The hotels themselves seem to be stuck in a time warp. The Panoramic, for instance, generally held to be the best of the bunch, has a gorgeous view of the vineyards but is rather dilapidated and has a breakfast to ignore (buy coffee and a croissant in one of the local cafés, instead). Book twin beds to avoid a sagging double.

On the other hand, food is excellent in two of the town's restaurants. La Pomme d'Or, not long open, is a hot tip among the locals (do book; it's small and extremely good value). The chef is a veteran of some fine restaurants, fulfilling an ambition to set up on his own, and his cooking is irreproachable. Grander and longer-established, but with an equally good reputation, is La Tour.

For a short, scenic trip leave Sancerre on the D955 towards Bourges, and turn right onto the D923 to Menetou-Râtel. Turn right off this road to reach **Chavignol**, where you can stop after the church at the tasting-room of **HENRI BOURGEOIS**. This is a fairly large family firm (there's a *négociant* arm, Laporte, run by a nephew-in-law) making reliable, good-quality wines including a Sancerre Rouge with plenty of depth.

The family seems to be taking over the village; tenth generation Bourgeois, Jean-Marc, has just opened a restaurant called La Côte des Monts-Damnés. The Monts-Damnés are local vineyard sites, damned because of how steep they are and difficult to work. Jean-Marc has served his apprenticeship in top French restaurants and puts his considerable expertise to good use. Don't miss the tagliatelle with the famous local goat's milk cheese, Crottins de Chavignol. (Another hot tip – remember, you read it here first.)

In the village square pick up signs proclaiming: 'Sancerre par les vignes – Panorama' and follow them up high through the vineyards along a narrow road (apparently one-way) overlooking spectacular views. This road brings you out on the D183. Head into Sancerre and turn right onto the D955, away from the river.

If you're interested in exploring the cheaper wines from the outlying villages, stay on the D955 and retrace the route mentioned at the end of the Loire Valley chapter (page 72) as far as Quincy. Two producers I'd recommend are **HENRY PELLÉ** in **Morogues** and **DOMAINE MARDON** in **Quincy** (details are given in the Sancerre and Pouilly Listings). Otherwise, take the D920 at the D955 roundabout, up past the Panoramic hotel on the road to Ménétréol. You'll find **DOMAINE JOSEPH MELLOT** on your right as you descend towards the river.

This estate also has a tasting-room on the main square in Sancerre, called the Auberge du Joseph Mellot, which offers a range of wines to taste with local specialities such as Crottins de Chavignol. At the cellars, on the other hand, you can see a forest of stainless steel and some fibreglass maturation tanks with adjustable lids, which sit on top of the wine forming an airtight seal no matter how much wine is in the vat.

This is a big company, making good wines – for a price. The Sancerre and Pouilly-Fumé cost from FF45 to FF66, but the wines from the outlying villages of Menetou-Salon, Quincy and Reuilly are lower priced at F34 each. From here, take the D920 to St-Bouize and then turn left onto the D59 to Pouilly.

Pouilly-sur-Loire was something of a gastronomic Mecca before the bypass was built but since then things have faded somewhat. Locals speak well of Le Coq Hardi (although it lost its Michelin star rating) and it can also provide accommodation. About 3km south of Pouilly, on the right off the N7, lies the Hôtel de Pouilly. Recently built, its well-equipped modern rooms are a real haven, and it serves an excellent breakfast. The hotel also has a restaurant, and when I was there it seemed as though Pouilly's entire work-force had descended for a good night out, with enormous seafood platters and steaks proving very popular.

Local producer **GUY SAGET** is a self-made man. His father, a small-scale winemaker, died suddenly when Guy was just 19, and he broke off his studies to take over the business, knowing at that time next to nothing about it. I don't think he's had a day off since, as he's laboured to build it up into the thriving vineyard holdings and *négociant* operation he runs today.

There's a small tasting-room on the main street of Pouilly and a larger one on the N7 south of town, where his headquarters are. Make an appointment to visit Saget's new project, the Moulin de Beauregard, in the next village south. He's restored this old windmill and created a tasting-room amid rows of barrels, as well as setting up art exhibition facilities. It's well worth a visit.

Back in Pouilly, between the N7 and the town centre, is the **TINEL-BLONDELET** estate, run by a young couple offering classic Pouilly-Fumé plus the results of various experiments with different styles of winemaking. There's also a good Pouilly-sur-Loire, proving that interesting wine can be made from the dull Chasselas grape.

Here, as so often, you'll find all manner of filtration equipment. Any unfiltered wine is worth seeking out – see for yourself what difference it makes. Just as I was leaving Pouilly, I met an American importer who rejoiced in having discovered a man producing unfiltered Pouilly-Fumé, just down the road from Tinel-Blondelet: Fabien Colin. Was he in when I called? Of course not. I don't know what the wines are like, but I mention the lead for what it's worth and I hope you strike lucky.

To complete the circuit, head north through Pouilly, and when you come to the turning for the N7 keep going instead towards Les Loges. It's a bumpy, potholed road but the view down across the valley is stunning. In Les Loges, follow signs for Sancerre or Cosne-sur-Loire through Bois-Gibault and Tracy-sur-Loire. When the road comes out on the outskirts of Sancerre you can head back into town on the D4 or take the N7 north and home.

Listings

When telephoning France from the UK, the number must be preceded by the digits 010 33. Producers are listed in wine route order, and hotels/restaurants by town or village according to the route. Accommodation prices are per room, meal prices are per head.

THE AUBE

Producers

Union Auboise
Domaine de Villeneuve,
10110 Bar-sur-Seine
Tel 25 38 30 65, Fax 25 29 73 21
Visitors' centre open Mon–Fri 9–12,
14–18 (provisional times);
cellar visits by appointment
Good English

André Drappier
10200 Urville
Tel 25 27 40 15, Fax 25 27 41 19
Open Mon–Sat 8–12, 14–18; closed lunch-time (definitely); cellar tour by appointment: 'phoning only half an hour beforehand will do'
Credit cards accepted
Good English

Domaine Michel Noirot
Clos St-Roch,
4 avenue Croix de Mission,
10340 Les Riceys
Tel 25 29 38 46, Fax 25 29 67 22
Visits by appointment Mon–Sun;
if possible book 1–2 days in advance
Some English
(good English from secretary)

Hotels and Restaurants
H Hotel   *R* Restaurant

Troyes
HR Hôtel la Poste
1–3 rue R-Poincaré, 10000 Troyes
Tel 25 73 05 05, Fax 25 73 80 76
Rooms FF350–490, Meals: La Table Gourmande FF135–185; Bistro de la Mer FF90–125

HR Royal Hôtel
22 boulevard Carnot, 10000 Troyes
Tel 25 73 19 99, Fax 25 73 47 85
Rooms FF265–500, Meals FF98–185

Bar-sur-Aube
HR Relais des Gouverneurs
38 rue Nationale, 10200 Bar-sur-Aube
Tel 25 27 08 76, Fax 25 27 20 80
Rooms FF270–290, Meals FF88–360

CHABLIS

Producers
Cave Coopérative La Chablisienne
8 boulevard Pasteur, 89800 Chablis
Tel 86 42 11 24, Fax 86 42 47 51
Open Mon–Sat 8–12, 14–18
(open in summer to 19.00),
Sun 9.30–12, 14–18
Credit cards accepted
Good English

Jean-Paul Droin
14 bis, rue Jean-Jaurès, 89800 Chablis
Tel 86 42 16 78, Fax 86 42 42 09
Visits (strictly) by appointment
Credit cards accepted
No English

Domaine René & Vincent Dauvissat
8 rue Emile Zola, 89800 Chablis
Tel 86 42 11 58
Visits by appointment;
closed Sun & during harvest
No English

Le Cellier Chablisien
7 rue Jules-Rathier, 89800 Chablis
Tel 86 42 15 64
Open Mon–Sun 9–12, 14–18
Good English

Domaine des Malandes
63 rue Auxerroise, 89800 Chablis
Tel 86 42 41 37, Fax 86 42 41 97
Open Mon–Fri 9–12, 14–19;
visits by appointment Sat
Credit card facilities to be introduced
Good English

Domaine Alain Geoffroy
4 rue de l'Equerre, Beines,
89800 Chablis
Tel 86 42 43 76, Fax 86 42 13 30
Open Mon–Sat 9–12, 14–18;
visits by appointment Sun
Credit cards accepted
Some English

Domaine de la Meulière
Fleys, 89800 Chablis
Tel 86 42 13 56, Fax 86 42 19 32
Open Mon–Sat 9–12, 14–18;
visits by appointment Sun
No English

Gilbert Picq & Ses Fils
3 route de Chablis, Chichée,
89800 Chablis
Tel 86 42 16 78, Fax 86 42 42 09
Open Mon–Fri 8–12, 14–18;
appointment preferred; visits (strictly)
by appointment Sat & Sun
Good English

Domaine Jean-Marc Brocard
Préhy, 89800 Chablis
Tel 86 42 45 76, Fax 86 41 45 79
Open Mon–Fri 8–18 incl lunch-time,
Sat 10–12, 15–19; closed Sun, but shop
in Chablis open 9–13
Credit cards accepted
Good English (except on Saturday!)

Bourgognes Bersan
20 rue de l'Eglise,
89530 St-Bris-le-Vineux
Tel 86 53 33 73, Fax 86 53 38 45
Visits by appointment
Some English

GAEC du Parc Verret & Ses Fils
7 route des Champs,
89530 St-Bris-le-Vineux
Tel 86 53 31 81, Fax 86 53 89 61
Open Mon–Sat 8–12, 14–19;
cellar visits by appointment
Good English

Caves de Bailly
Bailly, 89530 St-Bris-le-Vineux
Tel 86 53 34 00, Fax 86 53 80 94
Open for sales Mon–Fri 8–12, 14–18,
Sat & Sun: Jan & Feb 14.30–18, March–
Dec 10–12, 14.30–18; cellar open
April–Sept Mon–Sun 14–17 (small
charge for cellar visits; tastings FF9 per
glass, refundable on purchase)
Cellar tours in English

Léon Bienvenu
Rue Promenade, Irancy,
89290 Champs-sur-Yonne
Tel 86 42 22 51, Fax 86 42 37 12
Visits by appointment Mon–Sun 9–12,
14–18 (not Sun pm)
No English

Jean-Pierre Colinot
1 rue des Chariats, Irancy,
89290 Champs-sur-Yonne
Tel 86 42 33 25
Open Mon–Fri 9–12, 14–20, Sat 9–20
incl lunch-time, Sun 9–12
Some English

Hotels and Restaurants
H Hotel **R** Restaurant

Chablis
HR Hostellerie des Clos
Rue Jules-Rathier, 89800 Chablis
Tel 86 42 10 63, Fax 86 42 17 11
Rooms FF230–570, Meals FF160–400

H Hôtel l'Etoile
4 rue des Moulins, 89800 Chablis
Tel 86 42 10 50, Fax 86 42 81 21
FF140–250

R Le Vieux Moulin
Rue des Moulins
Tel 86 42 17 30
FF59–165

Beine
R Le Vaulignot
30 Route Nationale
Tel 86 42 48 48
FF98–235

Nitry
R La Beursaudière
Rue Hyacinthe Gautherin
Tel 86 33 62 51
FF71–190

Champs-sur-Yonne
R Les Rosiers
7 rue Dr Schweitzer
Tel 86 53 31 11
FF92–130

Vincelottes
HR Auberge Les Tilleuls
12 quai de l'Yonne,
Vincelottes,
89290 Champs-sur-Yonne
Tel 96 42 22 13, Fax 86 42 23 51
Rooms FF230–400, Meals FF98–280

SANCERRE AND POUILLY-SUR-LOIRE

Producers
Henri Bourgeois
Chavignol, 18300 Sancerre
Tel 48 54 21 67, Fax 48 54 14 24
Open Mon–Sat 9–12, 14–19, Sun &
public holidays 10.30–12.30, 15–17;
closed Jan & Feb on Sun
Credit cards accepted
Some English

Domaine Henry Pellé
18220 Morogues
Tel 48 64 42 48, Fax 48 64 36 88
Open Mon–Sat 9–12, 14–18
Some English

Domaine Mardon
Route de Reuilly,
18120 Quincy
Tel 48 51 31 60, Fax 48 51 35 55

Open Mon–Sat 8–12, 14.30–18;
appointment preferred
No English

Domaine Joseph Mellot
Route de Ménétréol,
18300 Sancerre
Tel 48 54 21 50, Fax 48 54 15 25
Cellars open Mon–Sat 8–18 incl lunch-
time; shop open March–Oct Mon &
Tues and Thurs–Sun 8–21
Credit cards accepted
Good English

Guy Saget
Route Nationale,
58150 Pouilly-sur-Loire
Tel 86 39 16 37, Fax 86 39 08 30
Tasting-rooms open Mon–Sun
8–12, 14–18
Moulin de Beauregard: visits by
appointment
Good English

Domaine Tinel-Blondelet
La Croix Canat,
58150 Pouilly-sur-Loire
Tel 86 39 13 83, Fax 86 39 02 94
Open summer Mon–Sun 8.30–12.30,
13.30–20; closes earlier in winter; closed
first week Sept & during harvest; no
appointment necessary for tasting,
appointment preferred for cellar visit
Credit cards accepted
Good English

Hotels and Restaurants
H Hotel   *R* Restaurant

Sancerre
H Le Panoramic
Rempart des Augustins,
18300 Sancerre
Tel 48 54 22 44, Fax 48 54 39 55
FF280–330

R La Pomme d'Or
Place Mairie (on Sentier Pédestre)
Tel 48 54 13 30
FF75–220

R La Tour
Nouvelle Place
Tel 48 54 00 81
FF98–280

Chavignol
R La Côte des Monts-Damnés
18300 Sancerre
Tel 48 54 01 72
FF95–140

Pouilly-sur-Loire
HR Hôtel de Pouilly &
   Restaurant Le Relais Grillade
(off N7, 3km south of Pouilly)
58150 Pouilly-sur-Loire
Tel 86 69 07 00, Fax 86 69 02 43
Rooms FF240–360, Meals FF82–155

HR Le Relais Fleuri &
   Restaurant Le Coq Hardi
42 avenue de la Tuilerie,
58150 Pouilly-sur-Loire
Tel 86 39 12 99, Fax 86 39 14 15
Rooms FF250–270, Meals FF100–240

Ferry Factfile

Of all the ways you can get across the Channel, which one is right for you? Sometimes it's clear that only one route is feasible. At other times there's a choice, for which you need more information. In the course of researching this guide I've travelled on most of the available crossings and the following is one woman's subjective response to what she experienced. I hope this information will help you make up your mind how to travel.

The crossings divide into three groups: those that deposit you at or near Calais, those that drop you in Holland or Belgium, and those that set you down somewhere along the Normandy coast. The short crossings operate frequently, the longer crossings perhaps only twice a day. Bear in mind with the longer routes that they may only let you on the ship an hour before sailing; it could be better to eat before you embark.

First, the crossing to **Calais**. This is easily the best of the shorter routes as far as roads are concerned on both sides of the Channel. The new M20/A20 dual carriageway takes you right up to the roundabout outside the port of **Dover**, and the computerized check-in takes a matter of minutes. You'll be given a lane number to follow; you park in that lane and board usually within 20 minutes. At Calais, the motorway again extends right up to the port – there's no quicker getaway.

Both P&O and Stena Sealink offer a service as frequent as every 45 minutes at peak times of the day, even in winter. Sealink ferries take 90 minutes to cross, P&O only 75. P&O has extra lounges, accessible on payment of a £6 supplement, where you can retire to if the ship is very full. Sealink, alas, is phasing out its free motorists' lounges; apparently it's too hard to keep out non-motorists.

Then there are the catamaran and hovercraft services run by Hoverspeed. These also cover the Dover to Calais route, with an additional SeaCat service from **Folkestone** to **Boulogne** (a much more pleasant option for a day trip, but less use if you need to put in any distance after landing as you have to cut across country to join the A26). The SeaCats are quicker than the ferries, taking 50 minutes, and the hovercraft claims just 35, although when I last travelled on the hovercraft, in a brisk Force 6, the crossing took nearly an hour. The stuffy craft heaved and banged about (the noise level is almost overwhelming) and people looked more than a little green.

The SeaCat, too, has an unnerving tendency to roll in even moderate seas. These vehicles may be faster (and loading and unloading is certainly very quick) but I'd really only recommend them for those with iron stomachs.

Sally Line also covers the same section of the Channel, but I don't think it's a contender. Access to **Ramsgate** is along a much slower road than the one to Dover, and from **Dunkerque** you either have to drive south to pick up the A26 at Calais or join it south of Lille. Although the motorway to Lille is toll-free, it's badly-surfaced and very congested with local traffic. Add to this the fact that the crossing time, at two and a half hours, is at least an hour longer than the Dover route, and it's clear that the timings just don't compare.

In addition – and I know it was only one journey – when I travelled with Sally Line the outward boat was cancelled altogether (wait another couple of hours for the next one or drive to Dover) and the return boat was delayed for 20 minutes. I also found port direction signs poor, check-in staff very fierce and the ship lacking in quiet, smoke-free areas for passengers to sit in. Sally Line offered to undercut any other company's crossing fare by £5, in 1993. If you add up the extra time it takes to get to both ports, and the extra crossing time, I think that comes out as needing more than a £5 price cut to compensate. All in all, it's not to be recommended.

What about the **Channel Tunnel**, running from **Folkestone** to just outside **Calais**? The idea is that the check-in is like a French *péage* or tollbooth: turn up, pay your money, join the queue for the next train. Although you can buy tickets in advance you can't book a particular train. They'd like (at present) to discourage advance booking, so there is no separate queue for ticket-holders; those with pre-paid tickets simply get in line with those buying tickets on arrival.

Then you have the choice of stopping to eat or buy duty-free goods (there's no shop or buffet on the train) or of going straight into the holding area to join the queue for the next train. Once you're in the holding area there's no escaping the queue and heading back to the service area (perhaps with one of those handy numbered tickets you get at delicatessen counters to keep your place). This, it is hoped, will not be a problem, with a crossing anticipated every 15 minutes in peak hours. The possibility of delays shouldn't be ruled out, however, until the system has become fully operational and trains reach maximum frequency.

The Tunnel offers a revolutionary way of crossing the Channel. It's fast and those with less than cast-iron stomachs don't need to worry about rough seas. Motorway connections are good at both ends – on the French side you are five minutes from the A26 just outside Calais.

Whether or not you fancy travelling this way, I believe the Tunnel has one enormous advantage over every other means of crossing – and that's because of Customs and Excise. When you cross by train, all Customs formalities are completed on the departure side. This doesn't make a great deal of difference when you're heading towards France, as French Customs officials don't seem to mind too much what we bring in. But anyone who's zoomed off the ferry in the UK port in double-quick time only to be brought to a standstill by a queue inching past stern-looking Customs officers will have cause to be thankful. With the Tunnel, this is an experience you undergo while you're waiting for the next train under the Channel and have nothing better to do, rather than after landing when you're itching to get onto the motorway and home.

For crossing to Holland and Belgium, the Olau Line has the shiniest ships and operates in some style between **Sheerness** and **Vlissingen**. The only disadvantage to this route is not of the company's making – it's the approach roads. From the M2 to Sheerness is half an hour of single-carriageway tedium, while from Vlissingen it's all motorway, but never the same one for very long.

Then there's **Harwich** to **Hook** (with Sealink) and **Felixstowe** to **Zeebrugge** (with P&O). These are handy crossings for avoiding the M25. Zeebrugge lies closer to the crossings to France but either is feasible, particularly if you're planning a longer holiday with an 'open-jaw' route.

North Sea Ferries, operating out of **Hull**, offers motorists from the north of England and Scotland the chance to avoid the long slog south – at a price. When costing the trip, however, bear in mind that, unique among ferry operators, dinner and breakfast are included in the fare. This leads to enormous pressure on the restaurant and my timing tip is to go in late for dinner. The ships sail at 6pm and arrive in **Zeebrugge** or **Rotterdam** at about 8am, so these are the only crossings which allow you to eat at a reasonable hour and get a decent night's sleep. Dinner service starts at 6pm, for families, and soon after it's bedlam; but hang on until 7.30 or, even better, 8pm, and the queues have usually subsided.

The other irritant for rugged individualists like me is that stewards herd you onto tables of eight to eat communally. I'm told by the PR people that individuals and couples can request separate tables, but to be on the safe side I'd have a strategy up your sleeve, such as friends about to join you or an unappealing personal habit. Breakfast queues are even worse, so hang back until 7.30am or so.

Of North Sea Ferries' two routes, the ships sailing to Rotterdam are bigger and newer and don't have those cabin-speakers through which to pump incredibly loud good-morning-campers messages as the Zeebrugge ships do. The crews are unfailingly friendly and the stabilizers, particularly on the boats to Rotterdam, are excellent. Although this port seems a long way north it can offer a very useful route through to Alsace.

Of the crossings for the Loire Valley, **Portsmouth** to **St-Malo** (taking nearly nine hours) is the best for getting a proper night's sleep. Brittany Ferries' boats are smart, the staff are sharp and the food is good. Brittany's crossings from **Portsmouth** to **Caen** (taking six hours) leave you bleary-eyed the next morning if taken overnight, and are better by day. The ship in fact docks at Ouistreham, 15km or so from Caen. (The company has a fiddly loading policy, which leaves you hanging around on the quayside while cars to the right and left sweep on board. It's all about achieving the right balance, apparently.)

Le Havre is better-placed for motorway connections than Caen, and routes to Le Havre often give you a longer night crossing.

The ferry routes I like least for getting to the wine regions are the ones to **Cherbourg**. The roads from Cherbourg are single-carriageway unless you drive round to Caen – in which case, why not take that crossing? It takes hours to get from Cherbourg to Angers or Tours, far longer than a motorway run would take. This is fine if you intend to pootle gently through the countryside from the moment you dock, but not if you want to get to your chosen area quickly.

I'm happy to say, however, that Stena Sealink has dropped its habit of turning you out of the cabins an hour before docking. Now they simply wake you up an hour or so beforehand, just like all the other companies. Apparently the old policy caused consumer unrest (I'll say).

Then there's the **Newhaven–Dieppe** crossing. Newhaven is now easy to get to thanks to the Brighton bypass, and Dieppe is by far the prettiest Channel port. If your schedule allows, you can spend a very pleasant first or last night here. Roads inland are not the fastest but you can still be on the outskirts of Paris in a couple of hours. The drawback is that disembarkation is slow, as you take it in turns to swing your car around in a tight little turning-circle to manoeuvre off. Also, seating accommodation is not always adequate when the ship is busy. Be prepared to pay a supplement to secure a seat.

A couple of final notes: Brittany Ferries crosses from **Plymouth** to **Roscoff**, which is handy for reaching the Loire if you live in south-west England, but a long slog otherwise; and Sally Line also runs a service from **Ramsgate** to **Ostend**.

Further Exploration

DIY VISITS

After following the wine routes described above, you may feel inspired to branch out and arrange your own visits. Perhaps you've enjoyed a particular wine bought in the UK and would like to trace it to its source.

The traditional method of making contact with a winegrower is to ask your wine merchant for an introduction. I did this when I first began to buy wine in France. My local merchant contacted several producers on my behalf. The results in France ranged from the distinctly off-hand to a VIP-style reception, proving that this method is no guarantee of a warm welcome but can be a good starting-point.

Most of us buy wine from the supermarket, so what would happen if you contacted Tesco, say, for an introduction to one of its suppliers? I asked all the major supermarkets and high street chains what their reaction would be if you asked for help. Most said that they would at least supply you with the grower's name and address, although few would go so far as to contact them on your behalf.

This is one area where the independent merchant can probably offer you more help than the high street wine shop or supermarket, but in most cases you are on your own in your investigations. You can also write to the address shown on a wine label; even if it's simply a name and a town, it should get through. Or you can write to the local wine committees. Some of them provide lists or even books of producers who sell direct to the public.

When you're in the region itself you'll drive past plenty of wine estates but how can you spot one worth visiting from the roadside? The first thing to check is that it does sell direct. Without signs such as *dégustation-vente* (tasting–sales), *vente directe* (direct sales) or *dégustation gratuite* (free tasting) you can't be sure that the public is welcome. A lack of these signs doesn't mean the producer definitely won't see you, but proceed with caution. The property may only receive visitors by appointment, and the winemaker may be busy; ask when it would be convenient to come back.

Next, size up the way the estate presents itself. I fight shy of places that proclaim themselves too loudly, with signs and displays such as barrels with bottles on top that shout at you from the roadside. This is pure prejudice on my part, but I prefer an estate which makes a more modest display.

After that, it's down to instinct, gut feeling, call it what you will. Is there a friendly welcome from whoever is on duty? Is the place clean? Are you offered a wine to taste in a decent-sized tasting-glass (shaped like an elongated tulip, called an ISO or INAO glass) or in little ones you can't get your nose into for a proper sniff? Is the winemaker showing you the wines you want or pushing something dearer? You can walk out at any time if the place doesn't look or feel right.

If you find yourself becoming totally hooked and want to brush up your French to have esoteric discussions with producers on the finer points of winemaking, you need *Lexivin/Lexiwine* by Paul Cadiau. This is a handy, pocket-sized dictionary giving translations into English and French of useful wine terms. If you want to know the French for crusher-destemmer, this book is for you.

When planning your own routes, the Michelin atlas gives the distances and journey times between major towns. If you devise a route following scenic back roads, remember to allow for the slow progress you'll make at, say, 50–55km per hour. You also need to watch out for the 'same-surname' problem among producers; there are often several winemakers with the same surname in one village, all scions of a single family. First names count.

If you want to stay longer than a few days in a region, consider self-catering accommodation. *Gîtes* are available in all the wine regions, but unfortunately the organizations in the UK which act as agents for them tend not to have much on offer amid the vines. Get round this by writing to the tourist information office in your chosen region and asking it to send you a list of what's available; then book direct. Many towns also offer a list of *gîtes* available locally.

You will also occasionally see signs advertising *chambres d'hôtes*. These offer bed and breakfast, and sometimes evening meals as well, usually eaten around a big table with the family – fine if your French is up to it. A few winemakers also offer bed and breakfast; the local tourist information office or Maison du Vin should be able to help you find them.

I believe you will enjoy the trip no matter what happens or how the visit is arranged. There's so much to discover in wine country, not only bargains from the château and vineyard but also friendly people, beautiful countryside, good food... Remember *la politesse*, have confidence and, above all, have fun!

Lexivin/Lexiwine by Paul Cadiau; self-published by Paul Cadiau in 1987, ISBN 2 907080 01 06; available from bookshops in the wine regions, Maisons du Vin etc.

INDEX

Abbaye de
  Ste-Radegonde **49**, 73
Accad, Guy 85-6
Aligoté 83, 91, 93, 95, 104,
  109
Aloxe-Corton 84, *89*, 98
Alsace 13, 14, 20, 22, 27, 38,
  142-71, *150*
Ambonnay 129, *131*, 134-5,
  140
Ambroise, Dom Bertrand 96,
  113
Amirault, Yannick 67, 76
Ammerschwihr 145, *150*, 163
Andlau *150*, 154-5
Angers 40, 42, 51, *52*, 53,
  75-6
Anjou 40, 42
Anjou Rouge 51, 55, 59
Anjou Sec 56
Anjou-Villages 51, 56-7, 58
Anjou-Saumur 44-5, 51-63,
  52, 74-6
appellation contrôlée (AC) 36
Arcelain, Virely 104
Arnould, Michel 134, 138
Aubance Valley 51
Aube 41, 121, 122-3, 172,
  173-80, *173*
Avize *131*, 140
Ay 124, *131*, 135-6, 140
Ayala 124, 135-6, 138

Bailly *183*, **186-7**
Bar-sur-Aube *173*, 174,
  178-9
Bar-sur-Seine *173*, 174, 175
Barr *150*, 154
Bas-Rhin 152-3
Basse-Goulaine *46*, 50, 51,
  74
battonage 156
Baudry, Bernard 66, 76
Baumard, Dom des 55-6, 74
Beaune 79, 83, 86, 87,
  98-103
Beauregard, Ch de 59-60, 75
Becker, Jean/Beck, Gaston
  160, 168
Beine *183*, 184
Benais *65*, 68
Bergères-lès-Vertus *131*,
  137, 141
Bergheim *150*, 158-9
Bethon *131*, 137
Bienvenu, Léon 187, 195
blanc de blancs 121
blanc de noirs 121
Blanck, Paul, & Fils 162, 168
Bollinger 140
Bonneteau-Guesslin 47, 73

Bonnezeaux 56
Botrytis cinerea 56
Bouilland *89*, 98
Bourgeois, Henri 189, 195
Bourgogne Aligoté 82-3
Bourgogne Aligoté de
  Bouzeron 109
Bourgogne Blanc 82
Bourgogne Côtes d'Auxerre
  186
Bourgogne Grand Ordinaire
  82, 95
Bourgogne Rouge 82, 91,
  95, 102
Bourgognes Bersan 186, 194
Bourgueil 41, 63, 64, *65*,
  67-8
Bouvet-Ladubay 62, 75
Bouzeron 83, *89*, 109
Bouzy 121, *131*, 135
Breton 64
Bricout 140
Briday, Dom Michel 110, 115
Brocard, Dom Jean-Marc
  185, 194
Brun de Neuville, Le 137,
  138, 176
Burgundy 13, 14, 22, 27, 37,
  78-116, *89*, 172, 181-8,
  183
Buxy 80, 112

Cabernet Franc **23**, 41, 51,
  62, 64, 71
Cabernet de Saumur Rosé 60
Cabernet Sauvignon 23, 51,
  62, 64
Castellane, De 139
Cave Coopérative La
  Chablisienne 182-3, 193
Cave Vinicole de
  Kientzheim/Kaysersberg
  162-3, 168-9
Caves de Bailly 186-7, 194
Caves de Cheilly 107, 114
Caves des Hautes-Côtes 103,
  114
Caves des Vignerons de Buxy
  112, 115
Cellier Chablisien, Le 184,
  194
Chablis 17, 36, 41, 79, 172,
  181-8, *183*, 193-5
Chagny *89*, 108
Chambertin 90, 91
Chambertin Clos de Bèze 90
Chambolle-Musigny *89*, 93
Chamirey, Ch de 111, 115
Champagne 13, 14, 23,
  38-9, 117-41, *131*, 172,
  173-80, *173*
Champalou, Catherine &
  Didier 70, 76-7
Champs-sur-Yonne *183*, 186

Champy Père & Cie 101-2,
  114
chaptalization 125
Chardonnay 23, 80, 82, 93,
  121, 137, 181, 186
Charmes-Chambertin 84, 90
Chassagne-Montrachet 84,
  105
Chasselas 144, 188, 192
Chassey-le-Camp *89*, 108
Château-Thierry *131*, 137,
  141
Chaudefonds-sur-Layon *52*,
  57
Chauveau, Dom Daniel
  66-7, 76
Chavignol 189-90, *190*
Cheilly-lès-Maranges *89*, 107
Chenin Blanc 23, 40, 51, 53,
  56, 64, 70, 71
Chéreau-Carré 47-8, 73
Chichée *183*, 185
Chinon 41, 63, 64, 65-7,
  65, 77
Chorey-lès-Beaune *89*, 96-7
Clevner 147
Clisson *46*, 47, 74
Clos de la Coulée de Serrant
  53-4, 74
Clos de Vougeot 78, 82, *89*,
  93-4
Clos de Vougeot, Ch du 93,
  100, 113
Clos Windsbühl 164-5
Clos Windsbühl 164-5
Closel, Dom du 54-5, 74
Clouet, André 135, 138
Colin, Fabien 192
Colinot, Jean-Pierre 187-8,
  195
Colmar 143, *150*, 165-6
Corton 97
Corton-Charlemagne 96, 98
Cot 71-2
Côte des Bar 174-80
Côte de Beaune 79, 83, 87
Côte de Beaune-Villages 83
Côte des Blancs 122, 137, 173
Côte Chalonnaise 79, 80, 83,
  87, 88, 108-12, 114-15, 116
Côte de Nuits 79, 87, 90
Côte de Nuits-Villages 83
Côte d'Or 79-80, 83, 85,
  88-108, 113-16
Coteaux d'Ancenis 51
Coteaux de l'Aubance 56
Coteaux Champenois 121
Coteaux du Layon 51, 55,
  57, 58
Cravant-les-Coteaux *65*, 66
Crémant d'Alsace 148, 161,
  163
Crémant de Bourgogne 83,
  187
Crémant de Loire 62, 71

cuvée 124
cuvée de prestige 122

Dauvissat, Dom René & Vincent 183-4, 194
Deiss, Marcel 159, 168
Delbeck 132-3, 138
Domptin 141
Dopff & Irion 160-1, 168
Drappier, André 177-8, 193
Droin, Jean-Paul 183, 194
Druet, Pierre-Jacques 68, 76
Dujac, Dom 91-3, 113
Dutertre, Dom 71, 77

Edelzwicker 148, 161
Eguisheim *150*, 166
en vrac 31
Epernay 63, 122, 129, *131*, 133, 137, 139-41
Epfig *150*, 156
Essoyes *173*, 179

fermentation 25-7
ferries 14-15, 197-202
Fesles, Ch de 58-9, 75
filtration 25, 27-8
fining 27
Fixin *89*, 90
Flagey-Echézeaux *89*, 95
Fleys *183*, 184-5
Folie, Dom de la 109, 115
Froehn 160

Gamay 51, 64, 71, 79, 82, 105
Gamay de Touraine 64
Garaudet, Jean 104
Gaudard, Dom 57, 74
Geoffroy, Dom Alain 184, 194
Germain, Dom Jacques 97, 113
Germain, Maison Jean 104, 114
Gevrey-Chambertin 84, 87, 88, *89*, 90-1, 96
Gewurztraminer 22, 144, 145, 147, 156, 157
Givry *89*, 109, 112
Golden Triangle, The 41, 79, 172-96
Grand Cru (Burgundy) 83-4, (Champagne) 123, (Alsace) 144-5, (Chablis) 181
Grand Vin de Bourgogne 84
Gratien, Alfred 63, 75, 125, 136, 138
Gratien & Meyer 61, 62-3, 75, 136
Gresser, Dom André & Rémy 38, 154-5, 168
Gros Plant du Pays Nantais 43, 49

Haie-Fouassière, La 46, 47
harvesting 38-9
Haut-Rhin 152-3, 156
Hautes Côtes de Beaune 79, 83, 87, 88, 96
Hautes Côtes de Nuits 79, 83, 87, 88, 96
Hinsingen 153
Husseren-les-Châteaux *150*, 166

Irancy *183*, 187
Itterswiller *150*, 155-6

Jambles *89*, 111
Jouy-lès-Reims *131*, 133
Juillot, Michel 111

Kaefferkopf 145, 163
Kaysersberg 144
Kientzheim *150*, 161-2
Kir 83
Klein aux Vieux Remparts 156-7, 168
Klevner 147
Klevner de Heiligenstein 147, 154
Klipfel, Dom 147, 154, 168
Krug 125
Kuentz-Bas 166, 169

Langlois-Château 62, 75
Layon Valley 51, 56
lees 27, 43
lieux-dits 145
Limeray *69*, 71
Loire Valley 13, 14-15, 36, 39, 40-77, *46*, 172

Maison des Vins de Nantes 47, 73
Malandes, Dom des 184, 194
malolactic fermentation 27
Mardon, Dom 190, 195-6
Maréchal, Dom Jean 110-11, 115
Mareuil-sur-Cher *69*, 71
Mellot, Dom Joseph 190-1, 196
Melon de Bourgogne 43
Menetou-Salon 72, 188, 191
Mercier 139
Mercurey *89*, 108, 110-11
Merrey-sur-Arce *173*, 175-7
Mesnil-sur-Oger, Le *131*, 137, 141
Meulière, Dom de la 185, 194
Meursault *89*, 104-5, 106
Meursault, Ch de 104, 114
Meyer, Jos 165, 169
Moët & Chandon 121, 122, 139

Moines, Dom Aux 54, 74
Montagne de Reims 122, 133-5
Montagny 112
Monthélie 96
Montlouis 41, 71
Montrachet, Le 105
Morey-St-Denis *89*, 91-3
Morogues 72, 190
Morot, Dom Albert 102-3, 114
Mortet, Dom Denis 90-1, 113
Moulin de Beauregard 191
Moulin de Chauvigné 55, 74
Mouzillon *46*, 48-9
Mozé-sur-Louet *52*, 56-7
Muré, René 166-7, 169
Muscadet 22, 27, 40, 43-4, 48, 49, 50
Muscadet des Coteaux de la Loire 43
Muscadet de Sèvre-et-Maine 43, 47
Muscat 144, 145, 147
Musée Animé du Vin et de la Tonnellerie, Chinon 65-6, 76
Musée de la Vigne et du Vin, St-Lambert-du-Lattay 57-8, 74
Mussy, Dom André 103-4, 114

Nantes 40, 42, 43, 44-6, 46, 73
négociant 80-1, 101
Nitry *183*, 185
noble rot 56
Noirot, Dom Michel 179-80, 193
non-vintage champagne 122, 127
Nuits-St-Georges 88, *89*, 95-6

oak barrels 25, 26
Obernai *150*, 153
Ostertag, Dom 156, 168
Ottrott *150*, 153

Pallus 66, 76
Palotte 186, 188
Parnay *52*, 63
Patriarche Père & Fils 100-1, 104, 114
Pays Nantais 40, 42, 43-50, *46*, 73-4
Pellé, Dom Henry 190, 195
Pernand-Vergelesses *89*, 98
Perrier-Jouët 140
Peters, Pierre 137, 138
Petit Chablis 181
Petite-Pierre, La 152, 153

Phylloxera vastatrix 80
Picq, Gilbert, & Ses Fils 185, 194
pigeage 67, 84–5, 187
Pineau de la Loire 40
Pinot Auxerrois 144, 147
Pinot Blanc 82, 144, 147, 156
Pinot Gris 144–6, 156
Pinot Meunier 121, 122
Pinot Noir 23, 79–80, 82, 84, 121, 144–5, 147–8, 174, 188
Piper-Heidsieck 139
Pommard 89, 103–4, 106
Pommard, Ch de 103, 114
Pommery 139
Pouilly-Fumé 188, 192
Pouilly-sur-Loire 41, 188, 190, 191–2, 195–6
Préhy 183, 185
Premeaux-Prissey 89, 96
Premier Cru (Burgundy) 83–4, (Champagne) 123, (Chablis) 181
press 25
Prieur, Dom Jacques 104–5, 111, 115
Prieur-Brunet, Dom 106–7, 114
Prudhon, Henri 105–6, 114
pruning and training vines 37–8
Puligny-Montrachet 84, 89, 105
Puy-Notre-Dame, Le 52, 59

Quarts de Chaume 55–6
Quincy 188, 190–1

racking wine 27
Reims 122, 129–32, 131, 139
remuage 119, 126
Renaudie, Dom. de la 71–2, 77
Reuilly 188, 191
Ribeauvillé 150, 159
Riceys, Les 121, 173, 179–80
Richou, Dom 51, 56–7, 74
Riesling 20, 22, 142, 144, 145, 146, 156, 157
Rigoles du Pin, Dom des 48–9, 73
Rilly-la-Montagne 131, 133
Rion, Dom Armelle & Bernard 95, 113
Riquewihr 150, 160–1
Roche-aux-Moines, La 54
Rochefort-sur-Loire 52, 55–6, 57
Roches-Neuves, Dom des 63, 75
Rodet, Antonin 104–5, 109, 111, 112, 115
Roederer, Louis 139

Rolly Gassmann 147, 158, 168
Romanée-Conti 95
Rorschwihr 150, 158
Rosé des Riceys 121
Rosiers, Les 52, 61, 76
Rully 89, 108, 109–10
Rully, Ch de 109, 111, 115

Saget, Guy 191, 196
St-Aubin 89, 105–6
St-Bris-le-Vineux 183, 186
St-Fiacre-sur-Maine 46, 47
St-Gengoux-le-National 112
St-Hilaire-St-Florent 52, 62
St-Hippolyte 150, 156–7
St-Jean 89, 111
St-Lambert-du-Lattay 52, 57–8
St-Martin 89, 111
St-Martin-d'Auxigny 72
St-Nicolas-de-Bourgueil 64, 67
St-Romain 87, 89, 106
St-Romain-sur-Cher 69, 72
St-Vincent, Dom 63, 75
Sancerre 20, 41, 42, 72, 172, 188–91, 190, 195–6
Santenay 79, 80, 89, 106–7
Saumur 41, 42, 51, 52, 58, 59–63, 76
Saumur Blanc 60
Saumur-Champigny 51, 62, 63
Saumur Rouge 60
Sauveroy, Dom du 58, 74
Sauvignon Blanc 20, 22, 41, 64, 188
Sauvignon de St-Bris 36, 186
Sauvignon de Touraine 64, 71
Savennières 51, 52, 53–6
Savigny-lès-Beaune 89, 98
Schoffit, Robert 169
sélection des grains nobles 145
Sélestat 150, 157–8
Sézannais 122
Sick-Dreyer 163, 169
Sonnay 65, 66
stainless steel vats 25–6
Strasbourg 152–3
sur lie 43, 44
Sylvaner 144, 148, 158, 160

taille 124
Targé, Ch de 63, 75
tasting 19–25
terroir 36–7
Thannenkirch 150, 158
Thénard, Dom 112, 115
Thouarcé 52, 56, 58
Tinel-Blondelet, Dom 192, 196
Tokay 144, 145, 146, 157
Tollot-Beaut & Fils, Dom 97, 98, 113

Tour, Ch de la 94, 98, 113
Touraine 41, 42, 64–72, 65, 69
Touraine-Amboise 71
Tours 42, 64, 68, 77
traditional method 123, 124–8
Troyes 173, 174–5
Turckheim 150, 164–5

Union Auboise 175–6, 193
Urville 173, 177–8

Vallée de la Marne 122, 136
Varrains 52, 63
VDQS 36
vendange tardive 145
Verret & Ses Fils, GAEC du Parc 186, 194
Vertus 131, 137, 141
Verzenay 131, 134
vieilles vignes 38
village wine 83
Villaine, A & P de 109, 114
Ville-en-Bois, La 46, 49
Vilmart & Cie 125, 133–4, 138
vin de pays 36
Vin de Pays du Jardin de la France 36
vin de table 35–6
Vincelottes 183, 188
vinification 25–8
vintage 38–9
vintage champagne 122, 127
Volnay 89, 104
Vosne-Romanée 89, 95
Vougeot 93, 95
Vouvray 41, 64, 68, 69, 70–1, 77

Westhalten 150, 166–7
Wintzenheim 150, 165

yield 38

Zellenberg 150, 159–60
Zind-Humbrecht 147–8, 164–5, 169